ArcGIS® 9

Geodatabase Workbook

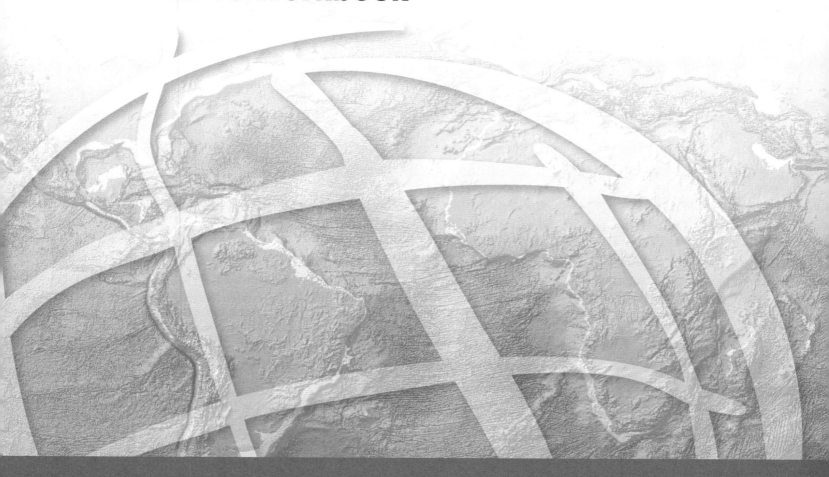

DATA CREDITS

Graphical Editing Map: Wilson, North Carolina
Universal Data Editor Map, Editing in data view and layout view map: Greeley, Colorado
Context menus and shortcut keys map: PFRA, Regina, Saskatchewan, Canada
Editing Tutorial Data: Wilson, North Carolina; Greeley, Colorado; PFRA, Regina, Saskatchewan, Canada
Map Topology Tutorial Data: U.S. Geological Survey in cooperation with U.S. Environmental Protection Agency, National Hydrography Dataset
Map Topology Tutorial Data: U.S. Geological Survey National Elevation Dataset Shaded Relief Image Service, published on the Geography Network
Topological Data Loading Tutorial Data: U.S. Geological Survey in cooperation with U.S. Environmental Protection Agency and Utah AGRC and REDCON

Creating and Editing Annotation Tutorial Data: U.S. Geological Survey National Elevation Dataset Shaded Relief Image Service, published on the Geography Network
Creating and Editing Annotation Tutorial Data: U.S. Geological Survey in cooperation with U.S. Environmental Protection Agency, National Hydrography Dataset

Creating and Editing Annotation Tutorial Data: National Atlas of the United States and the United States Geological Survey, Geographic Data Technology, Inc. (GDT), ESRI

CONTRIBUTING WRITERS
Bob Booth, Jeff Shaner, Andy MacDonald, Phil Sanchez, Rhonda Pfaff

Contents

1 Introduction   1

About this workbook   4

Building and editing geodatabases quick-reference guide   5

Tips on learning how to build and edit geodatabases   6

2 Quick-start tutorial   7

Exploring data in ArcCatalog   8

Editing attributes of geodatabase features   13

Finding and correcting topology errors   19

Making topological edits   26

Editing geometric network features   34

3 Editing GIS features   45

Exercise 1: Creating polygon features   47

Exercise 2: Creating line features   52

Exercise 3: Using a digitizing tablet   57

Exercise 4: Editing features   67

Exercise 5: Editing adjacent features with a map topology   75

Exercise 6: Importing CAD features   85

Exercise 7: Using geodatabase topology to clean up your data   90

Exercise 8: Using the Spatial Adjustment tool   122

Exercise 9: Using the Attribute Transfer tool   149

Exercise 10: Creating and editing annotation   158

4 Building geodatabases   173

Exercise 1: Organizing your data in ArcCatalog   175

Exercise 2: Importing data into your geodatabase   177

Exercise 3: Creating subtypes and attribute domains   182

Exercise 4: Creating relationships between objects   187

Exercise 5: Building a geometric network   189

Exercise 6: Creating annotation   194

Exercise 7: Creating layers for your geodatabase data   201

Exercise 8: Creating a topology   204

Exercise 9: Loading coverage data into a geodatabase topology   210

Glossary   229

Index   249

Introduction

1

IN THIS CHAPTER

- **About this workbook**

- **Building and editing geodatabases quick-reference guide**

- **Tips on learning to build and edit geodatabases**

Welcome to the ESRI® ArcGIS® *Geodatabase Workbook*. ArcGIS gives you advanced editing tools in ArcMap™ and feature behavior in geodatabases that allow you to create and maintain high-quality geographic data.

This workbook is divided into three parts: a quick-start tutorial, a section on editing, and a section on building a geodatabase. The quick-start tutorial provides a brief introduction to editing geodatabases and how feature behavior makes editing easier. The second part of the book provides exercises to help familiarize you with the feature creation and editing tools in ArcGIS. The third part provides exercises on building a geodatabase that will show you how to add the types of behavior illustrated in the quick-start tutorial to your own geodatabase.

This workbook tutorial lets you explore the capabilities of the geodatabase using ArcCatalog™ and ArcMap. An ArcEditor™ or ArcInfo® licensed seat of ArcMap is required to do the quick-start exercise. An ArcView® seat can be used to work through most of the editing exercises in the second part of the book. The geodatabase topology editing exercise requires an ArcEditor or ArcInfo seat. An ArcEditor or ArcInfo seat of ArcCatalog is required to do the geodatabase building exercises in the third part of the book.

The first two parts of this book focus on editing tools and techniques. ArcMap is the ArcGIS application for viewing, analyzing, and editing geographic information system (GIS) data, and it is the application you'll use most in this section. ArcMap provides powerful tools to create and edit the geometry of simple features. With ArcEditor or ArcInfo seats of ArcMap, you get additional tools and the capacity to edit features in geometric networks and geodatabase topologies. ArcEditor and ArcInfo seats of ArcMap also increase your productivity by enabling you to edit geodatabase features with subtypes, default values, attribute domains, and relationship classes. These make editing features and their attributes easier and less susceptible to error. Topology and network connectivity rules help you maintain the spatial integrity of your data.

ArcView	Comprehensive Data Use Simple Feature Editing
ArcEditor	ArcView Functions Plus Advanced Editing
ArcInfo	ArcEditor Functions Plus Comprehensive Geoprocessing

The third part of this book focuses on geodatabases and how to create them. In this part you will use ArcCatalog to load data into a geodatabase and add behavior to it. ArcCatalog is the ArcGIS application for browsing, storing, organizing, and distributing data.

ArcEditor or ArcInfo seats of ArcCatalog allow you to add behavior to your geodatabase to better model your data and help ensure that editing features is a quick and error-free process. A variety of behavior types can be created in ArcCatalog by defining subtypes, default values, attribute domains, relationship classes, topology, and network connectivity rules. Subtypes allow you to model several similar sorts of features in a given feature class. A roads

feature class could have subtypes for dirt roads, residential roads, and highways. Each could have different default values for the pavement type attribute, speed limit ranges, and rules regulating how each can be connected. Coded value and range attribute domains prevent and detect data entry errors. Relationship classes make it easy to access the attributes of related features and tables and help maintain the referential integrity of your data. Composite relationship classes and messaging within the geodatabase allow you to cause updates in one feature or table to be automatically reflected in other features. For example, when you move or change the name of a feature, its linked annotation will be updated to reflect the new position or content. When you create or delete a feature, another logically dependent feature can be automatically created or deleted.

You can create geometric networks to model networks of streams, pipes, or wires and enable tracing and network analysis. You can define connectivity rules that detect connections between incompatible components of a network, and you can specify whether network features, such as wires, should be physically split when features are attached to them along their length.

A geodatabase also allows you to define a set of topology rules that specify the spatial relationships that are allowable among features. Geodatabase topology helps you develop and maintain the spatial integrity of your data and lets you model geographic features and their spatial relationships more accurately. Geodatabase topology allows you to control what topology rules are imposed on your data. Some topology rules control relationships between features within a given feature class, while others control relationships between features of two different classes. You can choose whether a polygon feature class should be allowed to contain areas that overlap, as a record of wildfires or agricultural field treatments might, or whether overlaps should be prohibited, which could be desirable for landownership parcels or watershed boundaries. You can specify that all bus routes must follow streets or that storage tanks must fall within a spill containment berm area.

About this workbook

You can complete this workbook at your own pace, starting and stopping after each exercise or working straight through. Chapter 2, 'Quick-start tutorial', takes about 20 minutes to complete. Chapter 3, 'Editing GIS features', contains 10 exercises. Chapter 4, 'Building geodatabases', contains nine more exercises. Each exercise should take about 15–20 minutes to complete.

The study area for the quick-start tutorial and the chapter on building geodatabases is a hypothetical city. The data was created by ESRI using a database schema similar to that of the city of Montgomery, Alabama. The data is wholly fictitious and has nothing to do with the actual city of Montgomery. This information may be updated, corrected, or otherwise modified without notification. The data for the exercise on loading coverage data into a geodatabase topology is from the National Hydrography Dataset, published by the U.S. Geological Survey (USGS) in cooperation with U.S. Environmental Protection Agency (EPA) and Utah Automated Geographic Reference Center (AGRC) and REDCON. The watershed coverage, basin_utm, was fabricated for this exercise. This information may be updated, corrected, or otherwise modified without notification.

The data in the Editing folder is provided courtesy of the cities of Wilson, North Carolina, and Greeley, Colorado; by Prarie Farm Rehabilitation Administration (PFRA), Regina, Saskatchewan, Canada; and by the USGS and the EPA.

Building and editing geodatabases quick-reference guide

If you want more information about:	Refer to:	If you want more information about:	Refer to:
Editing a geodatabase: overview of subtypes, default values, attribute domains, topology, feature-linked annotation, geometric network, connectivity rules	*Geodatabase Workbook* 'Quick-start tutorial' *Editing in ArcMap* Chapters 2, 4, 9–14	Organizing data in ArcCatalog	*Geodatabase Workbook* Chapter 4, Exercise 1
		Importing data into a geodatabase	*Geodatabase Workbook* Chapter 4, Exercise 2 *Building a Geodatabase* Chapters 2, 3
Editing simple features in shapefiles or geodatabases	*Geodatabase Workbook* Chapter 3, Exercises 1, 2 *Editing in ArcMap* Chapters 2, 3	Creating subtypes and attribute domains	*Geodatabase Workbook* Chapter 4, Exercise 3 *Building a Geodatabase* Chapter 5 *Editing in ArcMap* Chapter 10
Using a digitizing tablet	*Geodatabase Workbook* Chapter 3, Exercise 3 *Editing in ArcMap* Chapter 5	Creating relationships between objects	*Geodatabase Workbook* Chapter 4, Exercise 4 *Building a Geodatabase* Chapter 6 *Editing in ArcMap* Chapter 11
Editing existing features	*Geodatabase Workbook* Chapter 3, Exercise 4 *Editing in ArcMap* Chapters 6, 7	Building a geometric network	*Geodatabase Workbook* Chapter 4, Exercise 5 *Building a Geodatabase* Chapter 7 *Editing in ArcMap* Chapter 12
Editing with a map topology	*Geodatabase Workbook* Chapter 3, Exercise 5 *Editing in ArcMap* Chapter 4	Creating annotation for your data	*Geodatabase Workbook* Chapter 4, Exercise 6 *Building a Geodatabase* Chapter 8 *Editing in ArcMap* Chapter 13
Importing computer-aided design (CAD) features	*Geodatabase Workbook* Chapter 3, Exercise 6 *Building a Geodatabase* Chapters 1, 3	Creating layers for your geodatabase data	*Geodatabase Workbook* Chapter 4, Exercise 7
Using geodatabase topology to clean up your data	*Geodatabase Workbook* Chapter 3, Exercise 7 *Editing in ArcMap* Chapter 4 *Building a Geodatabase* Chapter 4	Creating a topology	*Geodatabase Workbook* Chapter 3, Exercise 7, and Chapter 4, Exercise 8 *Building a Geodatabase* Chapter 4
Using the Spatial Adjustment tools	*Geodatabase Workbook* Chapter 3, Exercise 8 *Editing in ArcMap* Chapter 8		
Using the Attribute Transfer tool	*Geodatabase Workbook* Chapter 3, Exercise 9 *Editing in ArcMap* Chapter 8	Loading topological data	*Geodatabase Workbook* Chapter 4, Exercise 9 *Building a Geodatabase* Chapters 3, 4 *Editing in ArcMap* Chapter 4

Tips on learning how to build and edit geodatabases

If you're new to GIS, remember that you don't have to know everything about ArcCatalog, ArcMap, and geodatabases or how to extend the generic geodatabase data model to get immediate results. This workbook provides a set of tutorial exercises to familiarize you with editing and creating geodatabases.

Finding answers to questions

If you are like most people, your goal is to complete your tasks while investing a minimum amount of time and effort on learning how to use the software. You want intuitive, easy-to-use software that gives you immediate results without having to read pages of documentation. However, when you do have a question, you want to be able to find the answer quickly so you can complete your task. See *Editing in ArcMap* if you have questions about how to edit features in your GIS and *Building a Geodatabase* if you have questions on how to create your GIS.

About this book

This book is designed to teach you how to edit data in a geodatabase and how to create your own geodatabase. While this book does have some conceptual content, it assumes that you also have the books *Editing in ArcMap* and *Building a Geodatabase* available for more detailed discussion of concepts and directions for specific tasks.

Getting help on your computer

In addition to this book, the ArcGIS Desktop Help system is a valuable resource for learning how to use the software.

Contacting ESRI

If you need to contact ESRI for technical support, refer to 'Contacting Technical Support' in the 'Getting more help' section of the ArcGIS Desktop Help system. You can also visit ESRI on the Web at *www.esri.com* and *support.esri.com* for more information on the geodatabase and ArcGIS.

ESRI education solutions

ESRI provides educational opportunities related to geographic information science, GIS applications, and technology. You can choose among instructor-led courses, Web-based courses, and self-study workbooks to find educational solutions that fit your learning style. For more information, go to *www.esri.com*.

Quick-start tutorial

2

IN THIS CHAPTER

- **Exploring data in ArcCatalog**

- **Editing attributes of geodatabase features**

- **Finding and correcting topology errors**

- **Making topological edits**

- **Editing geometric network features**

In this quick-start exercise, you will use ArcMap to edit a geodatabase that models a part of a city. The geodatabase contains two feature datasets that model a water utility network and a planning department's land parcel records.

This geodatabase contains *subtypes*, *validation rules*, *relationships*, a *geometric network*, and a *topology*. You will use ArcMap to take advantage of the behavior built into this geodatabase. You can get more information about italicized terms in the glossary or consult the relevant chapters in *Building a Geodatabase* and *Editing in ArcMap*.

This chapter assumes that you have some familiarity with ArcGIS and that you are using an ArcEditor or ArcInfo licensed seat of ArcMap. The tutorial is intended to familiarize you with the basics of editing feature classes that have advanced geodatabase behavior.

Exploring data in ArcCatalog

Before you begin the tutorial, you must find the data and maps that you will need. You will use ArcCatalog to browse your data in this exercise.

Connecting to data

ArcCatalog lets you organize your local GIS data and maps in folders and easily access them through folder connections. You can access multiuser geodatabases by making database connections. When you look in a folder connection, you can quickly see the folders and data sources it contains. You will begin by creating a folder connection to the quick-start tutorial data.

1. Start ArcCatalog by either double-clicking a shortcut installed on your desktop or using the Programs list in your Start menu.

2. Click the Connect To Folder button.

3. Navigate to the EditingWithArcGIS folder on the local drive where you installed the tutorial data. The default installation path is C:\arcgis\ArcTutor\EditingWithArcGIS.

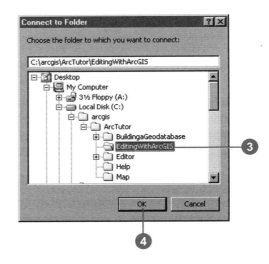

4. Click OK.

   Your new folder connection— C:\arcgis\ArcTutor\EditingWithArcGIS—is now listed in the Catalog tree. You will now be able to access all of the data needed for the quick-start tutorial through this connection.

Exploring your data

Before you begin editing the city geodatabase, you will explore the Landbase and Water feature datasets.

1. Click the plus sign next to the C:\arcgis\ArcTutor\EditingWithArcGIS folder.

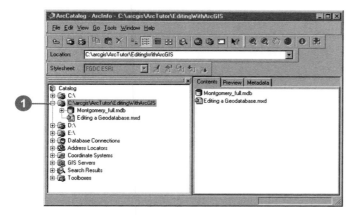

2. Double-click the Montgomery_full geodatabase and double-click the Landbase feature dataset to see the feature classes, relationship classes, and topology it contains.

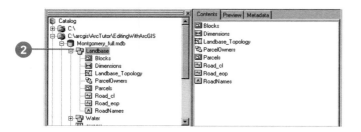

3. Click the Parcels feature class.

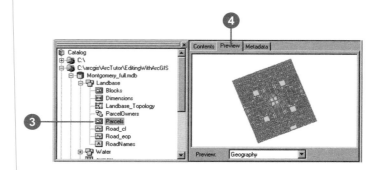

4. Click the Preview tab to preview the Parcels feature class geometry.

This feature class contains two types of parcel features, residential parcels and nonresidential parcels. They are rendered with different colors in the ArcCatalog Preview tab because they have been defined as separate subtypes in the geodatabase.

Subtypes are used to differentiate groups of features within a feature class that may share many of the same characteristics, yet have important differences in the typical values of some of their attributes or the role they play in the geodatabase. For example, a road feature class could have highway, arterial street, and residential street subtypes. All are types of streets, but highways might typically have four or more lanes and speed limits in the 45–70 mph range, while residential streets might always have two lanes and speed limits in the 15–30 mph range. The subtypes could have default values and range domains that reflect these differences.

Two subtypes within a feature class can have different topology and connectivity rules associated with them and often have different default values for certain attributes. Subtypes, default values, and attribute domains can help you ensure that your geodatabase contains high-quality attribute data. For more information about subtypes, see the 'Subtypes' chapter in *Building a Geodatabase*.

In this geodatabase, residential parcels have a default value of Residential for their zoning code, while nonresidential parcels have a default value of Commercial. Nonresidential parcels may be given another zoning code value, but since many of the nonresidential parcels are commercial, the default was set to Commercial as a convenience for the geodatabase editors.

5. Click the owners table in the geodatabase.

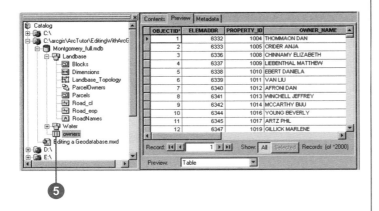

Notice how the Preview type automatically changes to Table and displays the table's records. This table contains the owner information for the Parcels feature class.

ParcelOwners is another type of geodatabase object, a relationship class. Relationship classes store information about how spatial objects, such as feature classes, or nonspatial objects, such as tables, are related to other objects within a geodatabase. ParcelOwners links the Owners table to the Parcels feature class. When you edit the parcels in ArcMap, you can view and edit the related data in the Owners table. For more information about relationship classes, see the 'Relationship classes' chapter in *Building a Geodatabase*.

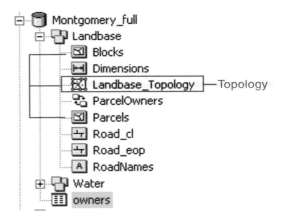

Landbase_Topology is a topology in the dataset. It provides rules that structure how the polygon features in the Parcels feature class can be spatially related to each other and how one subtype of Parcels can be related to one subtype of Blocks. Topologies help you maintain high-quality spatial data in your geodatabase. For more information about topologies, see the 'Topology' chapter in *Building a Geodatabase*.

6. Double-click Water.

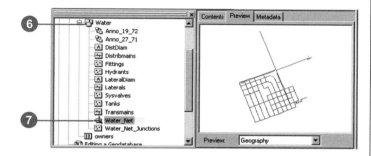

This dataset also contains relationship classes, annotation, and feature classes.

7. Click Water_Net.

Water_Net is a geometric network, another type of topological relationship, between the feature classes in this dataset. Geometric networks allow you to model networks of edges and junctions, such as the pipes and valves in a water system or the wires and switches in an electrical power grid. They let you conduct connectivity traces and flow analyses on the features in the network and provide some special editing functionality that is useful for networks. For more information about geometric networks, see the 'Geometric networks' chapter in *Building a Geodatabase*.

A relationship class, Anno_19_72, links a set of annotation to the Laterals features. If a water lateral is edited, the corresponding piece of annotation will be updated.

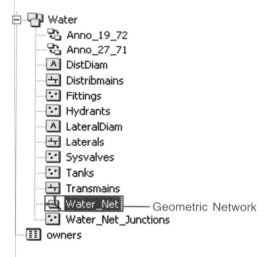

8. Click Editing a Geodatabase.mxd.

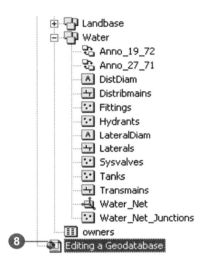

This is a map that you will use to edit the geodatabase objects you've been exploring. For more information about maps, see *Using ArcMap*.

In this section, you've explored the contents of the EditingWithArcGIS folder. In the next section, you will begin to do some advanced attribute editing on this geodatabase.

Editing attributes of geodatabase features

Imagine you work for the city planning department, and you have been asked to update the attributes of some parcels. You will edit attributes of geodatabase feature classes, edit values in a table connected to a feature class by a relationship class, and change the subtype of a feature.

Opening a map and starting to edit

1. Start ArcMap by double-clicking Editing a Geodatabase.mxd.

ArcMap starts, and you see a section of the city. You are going to edit some features on this map, so you'll need to add the Editor toolbar and the Topology toolbar to the map.

2. Click View, point to Toolbars, and click Editor.

3. Click View, point to Toolbars, and click Topology to add the Topology toolbar.

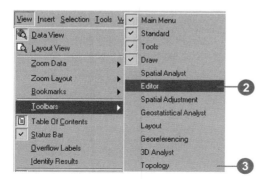

The Editor and Topology toolbars appear.

4. On the Editor toolbar, click Editor and click Start Editing.

Visiting a bookmarked area

Now you'll zoom to an area that has been defined by a spatial bookmark in the map and select some features to edit.

1. Click View, point to Bookmarks, and click EditParcel.

2. Click the Select Features tool.

3. Select a group of light green office parcels by dragging a box around them.

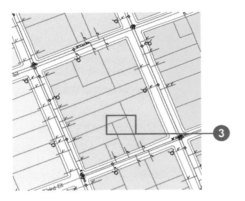

Viewing and editing values in a related table

Now you'll edit the Owners table, which is related to the Parcels feature class by the Parcel Owners relationship class.

1. Click the Attributes button on the Editor toolbar.

The Attributes dialog box now appears with a list of the selected parcels' PROPERTY_ID values. The attribute values of the first selected parcel are displayed on the right panel.

Each parcel has a plus sign next to it. You can navigate to the related row in the Owners table from each parcel.

2. Double-click the feature ID of parcel 4381 (it may not be the first in the list).

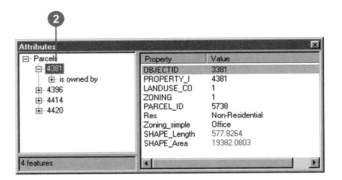

The database designer decided that a logical label for related fields in the Owners table, when viewed from the Parcels attributes, is 'is owned by'. You can specify such labels when you create a relationship class.

3. Click the plus sign next to 'is owned by'.

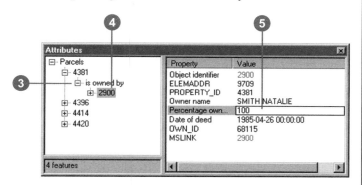

The identification number of the record in the Owners table that is related to—owns—this parcel is displayed under the 'is owned by' label.

4. Click the Owner Object identifier, 2900.

You are now viewing a record in the Owners table in the geodatabase. The attributes of the owner of this parcel are listed on the right panel. Some of the field names that are shown in this window are aliases instead of the true field names. Aliases are created by the geodatabase designer to make the usually short and sometimes cryptic database field names easier to read and understand. In this case, for example, one of the geodatabase fields is called OWNER_PERCENT. The alias 'Percentage ownership' was created to provide a more understandable label for the field in the Attributes window.

You can edit the values for this owner's attributes easily using the Attributes window.

5. Click the value for Percentage ownership and type "100".

6. Press Enter.

You have used the ParcelOwners relationship class to find the owner for a selected parcel feature and to edit that owner record in the related geodatabase table. Relationship classes can also be used to link two features or tables to each other or to link annotation to features. The geodatabase lets you use the relationship class to easily navigate between related objects and to maintain the referential integrity of the database.

Editing the subtype and an attribute of a feature

Now you'll edit the Parcels feature class. You will change the subtype of a parcel and also edit an attribute of a parcel.

1. Click the PROPERTY_ID of parcel 4381 in the Attributes window selection list.

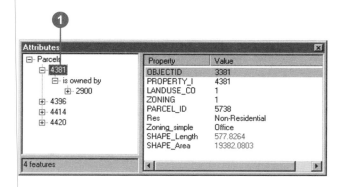

When you first viewed the parcel feature class in ArcCatalog, the features were drawn in two different colors because there are two subtypes of parcel. On this map the parcels are rendered using their Zoning_simple attribute rather than their subtype. Each parcel subtype has different default values defined for its Zoning_simple field. You will change the subtype of a parcel and see how other fields are updated with a new default value.

2. Click Non-Residential in the Value column to the right of the Res attribute.

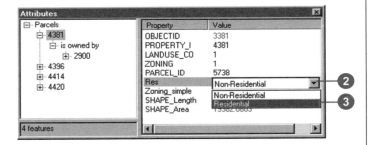

The Attributes window gives you a dropdown list that will let you select one of the two possible values for this field.

3. Click Residential in the list of two values.

This field is associated with a coded value *attribute domain* in the geodatabase. Coded value domains allow you to edit more quickly and accurately because you can pick from the list of predefined permissible values. There's no need to type the data into the field, and there's no possibility of entering a typo.

The attribute stored in this field is also the code that identifies which subtype the feature belongs to. Notice that when you changed the parcel's subtype attribute to Residential, the subtype of the parcel immediately changed. The value of the Zoning_simple attribute also

changed, as you can see in the Attributes window and on the map. This is because Residential is the default value for this attribute of parcels of the Residential subtype.

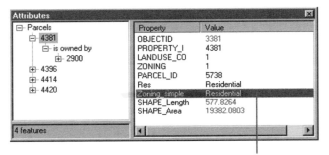

New attribute value from default value of Residential subtype

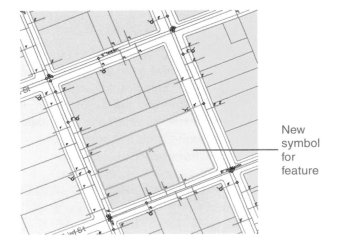

New symbol for feature

Next, you'll edit another parcel's subtype and attributes.

4. Click the PROPERTY_ID of parcel 4396 in the Attributes window.

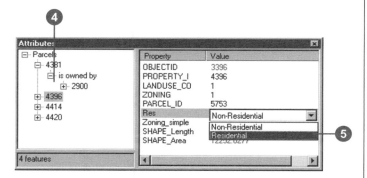

5. Click Non-Residential in the Value column to the right of the Res attribute and click Residential.

Notice that the Zoning_simple field is again updated with the default value, Residential.

6. Click in the Value column for the Res attribute and click Non-Residential to change the parcel's subtype back to Non-Residential.

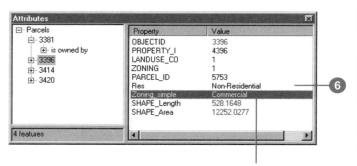

New value for Zoning_simple field

Notice that the Zoning_simple field is updated again, but now it has a new value—Commercial. The feature's symbol on the map is also a new color.

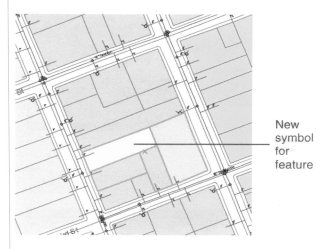

New symbol for feature

When the geodatabase was designed, it was decided that most new parcel features of the Non-Residential subtype would probably be commercial property, so Commercial was made the default value for nonresidential parcels.

Just because a parcel is nonresidential does not mean that it must have the Zoning_simple code Commercial. This parcel has been reclassified by the planning department as Manufacturing. You will update the Zoning_simple code to its new value.

7. Click Commercial in the Zoning_simple Value column and click Manufacturing.

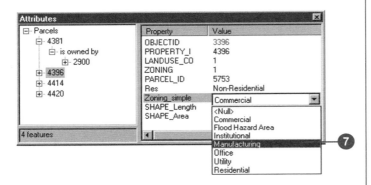

8. Close the Attributes dialog box.

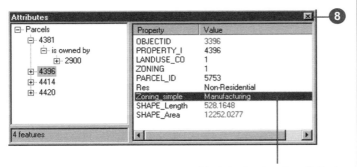

Updated value for attribute

You have updated the parcel's zoning code in the geodatabase and have seen how default values and coded value domains can make editing feature attributes quick and easy.

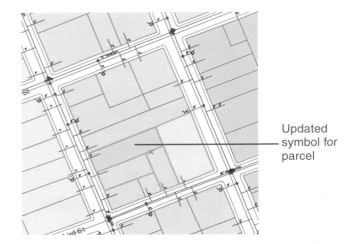

Updated symbol for parcel

In the next section you will examine the results of your edits on the feature dataset's topology, Landbase_Topology.

Finding and correcting topology errors

Now you will check the edits you've just made to find out if they violate the topology rules defined for these features.

A geodatabase topology defines a structured set of permissible spatial relationships between features within a subtype or feature class or between features in two subtypes or feature classes. These relationships are specified by topology rules when the topology is created. There are many possible topological relationships that could be important for a geodatabase, so ArcGIS allows you a great deal of flexibility in defining topological relationships. The Topology toolbar provides tools to help you find and correct topology errors and also provides editing tools to help you avoid creating topology errors when editing features in a topology.

Validating topology edits

Although you haven't changed the geometry of any features, you have changed the subtype of a couple of features. If a subtype of a feature class is specified in a topology rule, changing the subtype can create topology errors.

1. On the Topology toolbar, click the Validate Topology In Current Extent button.

The topology is validated within the area that is currently visible on your map.

Validating a topology can sometimes take some time to complete, especially if you have made a large number of edits, you are working on large or complex datasets, or you have many topology rules. Validating the current extent saves time when you are trying to locate errors in a specific area.

The topology validation process identified an error within the area you've just been editing and marked it with a red error feature. Red is the default color for error features, although you can change the way they are symbolized.

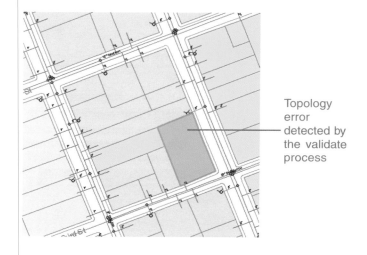

Topology error detected by the validate process

Examining topology properties

Now you'll investigate the properties of this topology to identify what the problem is. The Topology layer lets you view topology errors, as well as other information about the topology, in ArcMap.

1. In the ArcMap table of contents, right-click the Landbase_Topology layer and click Properties.

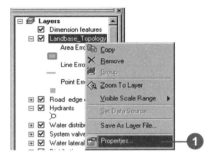

The Layer Properties dialog box for the topology layer opens.

2. Click the Feature Classes tab to see what feature classes in the dataset participate in the topology.

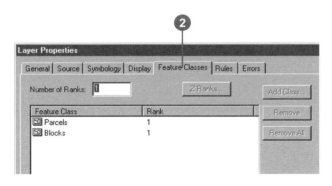

The Parcels feature class that you've just edited is one of two feature classes that participates in the topology; Blocks is the other.

3. Click the Rules tab to see which topology rules may have been violated by your edits.

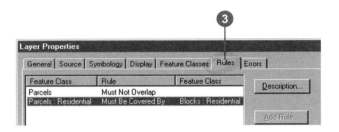

The rules of the topology are listed here. A topology could be created with no rules or with as many as a dozen, or more, depending on the complexity of your data model. The first rule in the list means that features within the feature class Parcels are bound by the Must Not Overlap rule. Parcels that overlap—for example, because of digitizing errors—will be discovered when the topology is validated. This rule does not involve a second feature class, so the second feature class column is empty.

Since you didn't edit any geometry, you're unlikely to have violated the Parcels Must Not Overlap rule. However, the second rule, Parcels: Residential Must Be Covered By Blocks: Residential involves the Residential subtype of the Parcels feature class, which you did edit. It states that Residential subtype features in Parcels must be covered by Residential subtype features in Blocks.

4. Click the row for the rule Parcels: Residential Must be Covered By Blocks: Residential.

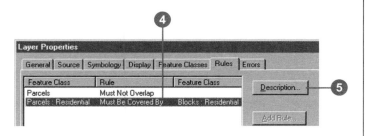

5. Click Description.

A dialog box appears with a brief description of the topology rule.

6. Uncheck Show Errors.

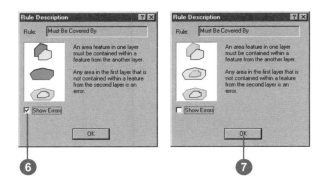

You can check and uncheck the Show Errors box to compare cartoon examples of features and the topology errors that they would produce. The red parts of the graphic represent error features.

7. Click OK.

8. Close the Layer Properties dialog box for the topology layers.

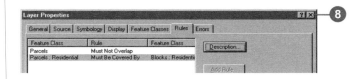

Next you'll use another method to explore topology errors.

Inspecting topology errors

Now you'll examine the errors in the topology using the Error Inspector.

1. Click the Error Inspector button on the Topology toolbar.

The Error Inspector window appears. You can allow it to float on the map, or you can dock it to the ArcMap application frame.

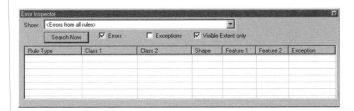

The Error Inspector will selectively show the errors where this rule is violated.

2. Click the Show dropdown list to choose what types of errors to display and click Parcels: Residential - Must Be Covered By - Blocks: Residential.

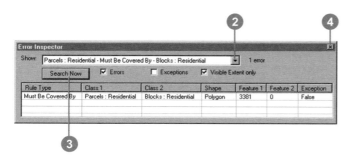

3. Click Search Now.

   The Error Inspector shows the error that is visible in the current extent.

   You can also use the Error Inspector to find all errors, regardless of their type or whether they are in the visible extent, or you can use it to find exceptions to topology rules. An exception is an error feature that has been marked as representing a valid exception to a topology rule.

4. Close the Error Inspector dialog box.

Fixing topology errors

In this feature dataset the Blocks feature class represents city blocks. These features have been created simply for demonstration purposes for this tutorial. Blocks have a subtype field that codes them as either Residential or Non-Residential. The Residential block features could be used by the Planning and Zoning office to track whether a given block has parcels that are used for housing. This information could then be used for business permitting purposes or for consideration in the zoning variance review process.

The topology rule Must Be Covered By ensures that residential parcels must be covered by, or fall within, Block features that are marked as residential. You will turn on the Block layer and look at the situation.

1. In the table of contents, check the Blocks layer.

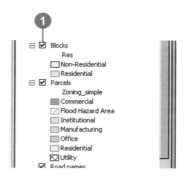

The Blocks layer is partly transparent, so you can see the parcel features through the blocks. The block that contains the error feature is a Non-Residential block. The first Parcel feature that you edited was originally nonresidential. When you edited it, you switched it to the Residential subtype, which triggered this topology error.

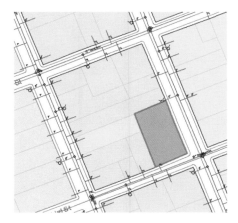

There are several possible ways to deal with this topology error. These include:

- Delete the residential parcel feature.

- Create a new block feature that covers just the residential parcel.

- Mark the error as an exception.

- Ignore the error.

- Change the subtype of the Block feature to Residential.

- Change the subtype of the Parcel feature to Non-Residential.

The correct choice would depend on the planning department's strategy for maintaining the Block and Parcel feature classes. Deleting the parcel is, in this case, not an option. Creating a new special Block feature would not be in accordance with the department's system of monitoring blocks with housing, nor would marking the error as an exception or simply ignoring it. The two most viable options are changing the subtype of the block to Residential or returning the subtype of the parcel to Non-Residential.

Let's assume that the original edit was correct and that this parcel really was supposed to be reassigned to the Residential subtype. It follows that the block should be changed to reflect its new status as a block containing a residential parcel.

2. Click the Select Features tool.

3. Click the block feature at the error feature.

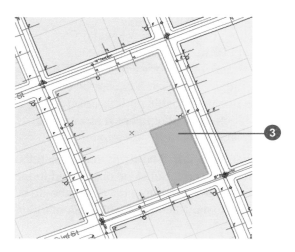

The block is selected.

4. Click the Attributes button on the Editor toolbar.

The Attributes window appears.

5. Click in the Value column beside Residential and click Residential in the dropdown list.

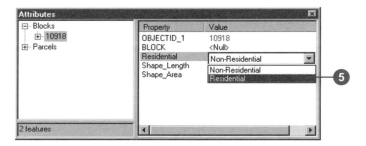

The block changes subtype to Residential, and the symbol for the block is updated on the map.

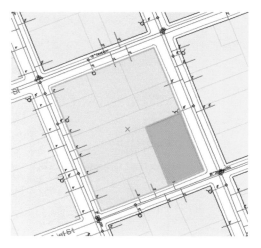

6. Click the Validate Topology In Current Extent button and close the Attributes dialog box.

The part of the topology visible on the map is validated, and since there is no longer a violation of the topology rule, the error is removed.

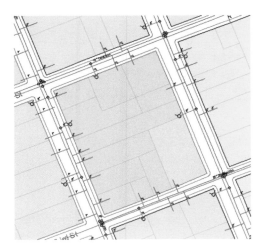

In this exercise you used the topology to maintain a specific spatial relationship between subtypes of the Parcel and Blocks feature classes. In the next exercise you will use the Topology Edit tool to edit a boundary shared by two features.

Making topological edits

Imagine you've been asked to move a parcel boundary to update the planning department's database. You will use the Topology Edit tool to edit the two features that share this boundary. The Topology Edit tool works on parts of features, called edges and nodes. Edges are line segments that define part of a line or part of a polygon boundary. Nodes are the endpoints of topology edges, but they can also be introduced along an edge to provide a convenient point to which to snap. Edges and nodes may be shared by several features in multiple feature classes. In this exercise you will move an edge that represents the boundary shared by the two parcel features. You will create two temporary topology nodes to make it easier to move the edge to the new location.

Preparing to edit the parcels

First, you'll need to turn off the Blocks layer, so you don't inadvertently edit the Block feature, then zoom in to the area where you'll be editing.

1. Uncheck Blocks.

2. Click the Zoom In tool.

3. Click and drag a box around the southern half of the block of parcels that's centered in the display on the map.

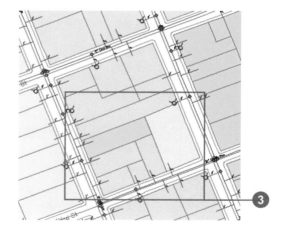

4. Right-click Parcels and click Label Features.

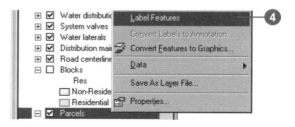

The northern boundary of parcel 4414 needs to be moved 30 feet south of its current position. You will create temporary topology nodes along the parcel's east and west boundaries and snap the north boundary to the new location.

5. Click Editor and click Snapping to set up the snapping environment.

You can snap to different parts of features, the edit sketch, or to topology nodes. You'll set the snapping environment to snap to topology nodes.

6. Check Topology nodes.

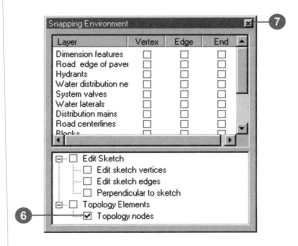

7. Close the Snapping Environment dialog box.

Now you'll change the way the topology nodes are drawn to make editing the parcel boundary easier.

8. Click Editor and click Options.

9. Click the Topology tab.

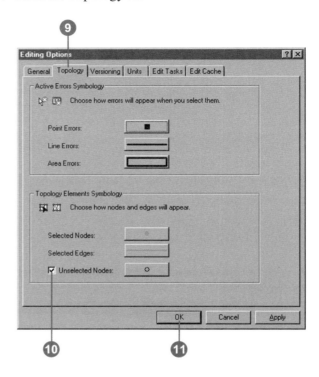

10. Check Unselected Nodes.

Normally, ArcMap shows the selected topology edges and nodes but not the unselected nodes. Since you will be snapping the edge to unselected nodes, it will be useful to be able to see them.

11. Click OK.

Editing the parcels

Now you'll use the Topology Edit tool to split the east and west boundaries to create topology nodes. You'll also check which parcels share the north boundary, then you'll be ready to move it.

1. Click the Topology Edit tool.

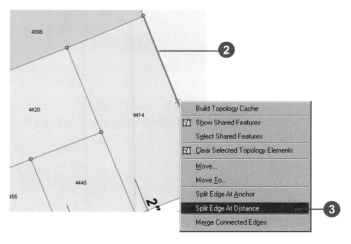

2. Click the eastern boundary of parcel 4414.

   The boundary edge is selected and changes color.

3. Right-click the selected edge and click Split Edge At Distance.

The edge now has arrows to show what direction it points. When you split an edge, you need to know which end is the beginning of the edge. The arrows point from the beginning to the end of the edge.

The topological relationships between the features in the current map extent are discovered by the Topology Edit tool when you start editing with the tool and when you rebuild the topology cache. Since these relationships are discovered on the fly and are not stored, the direction of an edge may vary between edit sessions, depending on the current map extent.

4. Look at the arrows on the edge. If they point south, type "30" in the Split text box and press Enter. If they point north, type "30" in the Split text box, click From end point of edge, and press Enter.

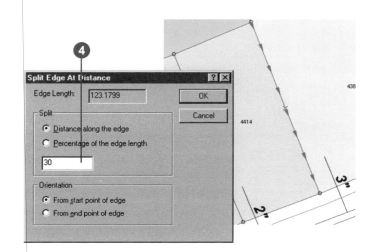

A new topology node is inserted at 30 feet from the north end of the edge.

5. Click the west edge of parcel 4414.

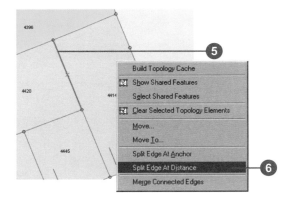

6. Right-click the west edge and click Split Edge At Distance.

7. Look at the arrows on the edge. If they point south, type "30" in the Split text box and press Enter. If they point north, type "30" in the Split text box, click From end point of edge, and press Enter.

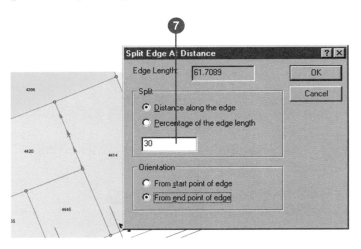

A second new topology node is inserted at 30 feet from the north end of the edge.

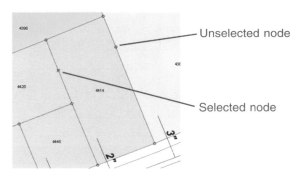

Unselected node

Selected node

The new topology nodes you added will allow you to snap the northern, shared edge of the parcel to its new location.

Now that both edges have had topology nodes added, you will be able to snap the boundary to the topology nodes. Before you move the edge, you'll check to see which features share it.

8. Click the boundary between parcel 4396 and parcel 4414.

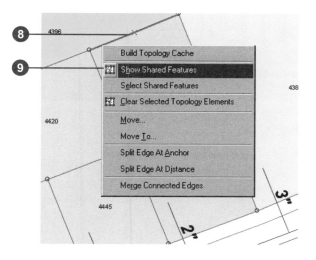

9. Right-click and click Show Shared Features.

10. Click the plus sign beside Parcels.

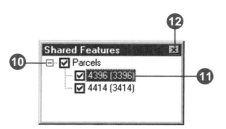

The Shared Features dialog box shows the features that share a selected topology element. This edge is shared by features 4414 and 4396 in the Parcels feature class.

11. Click 4396.

The parcel flashes on the map.

12. Close the Shared Features dialog box.

Next you will move the shared edge.

Moving the shared edge and nodes

The endpoints of this edge are topology nodes that are shared by these two parcels but are also shared by some other parcels. To move the endpoints of this edge, you will need to select the nodes, along with the edge, and split–move them. A split–move breaks the topological association between a selected node and unselected edges.

1. Hold the N key and drag a small box around the node at the eastern end of the edge.

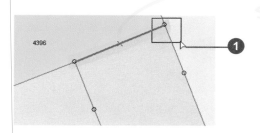

The topology node is added to the selection. Holding the N key allows you to select a topology node without selecting any more nearby edges.

2. Move the pointer over the selected node.

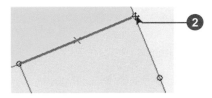

3. Press the S key with the pointer over the node.

The pointer changes to indicate that you can split–move this node. A split–move breaks the topological association between the node and unselected edges and allows you to move an endpoint of an edge that is shared by other features.

4. While holding the S key, click the node and drag it southeast until it snaps to the new topology node you created, then drop the node.

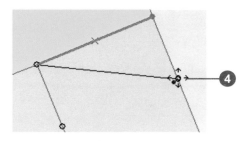

5. Hold the N key and drag a small box around the node at the western end of the edge.

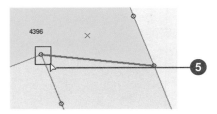

6. Move the pointer over the selected node.

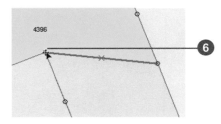

7. Press the S key with the pointer over the node.

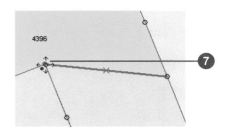

Now you can split–move this node to the new location.

8. While holding the S key, click the node and drag it southeast until it snaps to the new topology node you created, then drop the node.

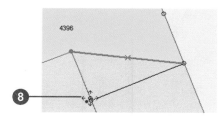

The shared parcel edge is moved to the new location. Because you split–moved the nodes at the endpoint of the edge, the corner of the parcel that did not share the edge (4420) was not modified.

9. Click the Validate Topology In Current Extent button.

The edits you've made to the parcels are checked against the topology rules. Because no rules were violated by the edits, no errors are found.

You have edited the attributes and geometry of some geodatabase features that participate in a topology. Next you'll save your edits.

Saving your edits

Now that you've completed editing the parcels, you should save your edits.

1. Click the Editor menu and click Save Edits.

The edits are saved to the geodatabase. In the next section, you'll edit some geometric network features.

Editing geometric network features

Imagine that you work for the city water department. You've been asked to update the geodatabase to show the new position of a fire hydrant that has been moved and to add another hydrant and its associated pipes and fittings. The hydrants are connected to the city water system, which is modelled using a geometric network in the geodatabase. A geometric network is another sort of topological relationship that the geodatabase can maintain among feature classes. Just as you can edit edges and nodes shared by multiple features in a topology, a geometric network allows you to edit network edge and junction features and maintain network connectivity between them.

1. Click View, point to Bookmarks, and click EditHydrant.

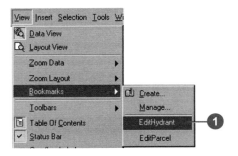

You will move the hydrant to the center of parcel 4054.

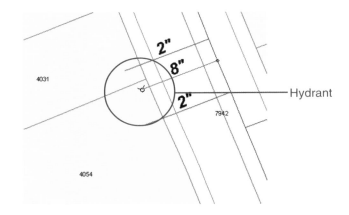

Moving a fire hydrant feature

This fire hydrant feature is a part of the geometric network. It is connected to the rest of the network by a hydrant lateral feature, a subtype of the water lateral feature class. You will see that network connectivity is maintained when the hydrant feature is moved.

First, you will change the selectable layers from all layers to Hydrants. This will make it easier to move the hydrant.

1. Click Selection and click Set Selectable Layers.

2. Click Clear All. You will change the selectable layers from all layers to only Hydrants.

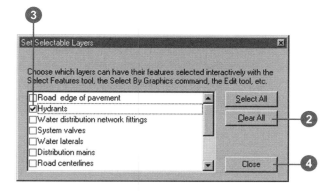

3. Check the Hydrants layer.
4. Click Close.

5. Click the Edit tool.

6. Drag a box around the fire hydrant.

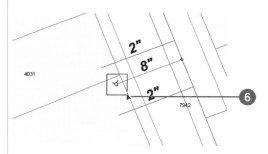

The fire hydrant should now be selected, but no other features are selected.

7. Click and drag the selected hydrant to the southwest, toward the middle of the parcel, then drop the hydrant into its new position.

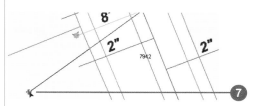

When the hydrant was moved, the lateral stretched to maintain its connectivity with both the hydrant and the valve. This is an example of how ArcGIS maintains network topology during editing.

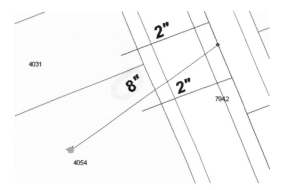

Also notice that the annotation for the lateral moved to fit the new location of the lateral. The annotation feature is linked to the lateral feature by a geodatabase relationship class.

Creating a new hydrant lateral

Now you will add a new hydrant lateral to a distribution main in the water network. This task will involve a combination of network editing, connectivity rules, attribute rules, and feature-linked annotation.

1. Click Selection and click Clear Selected Features to deselect the hydrant you just moved.

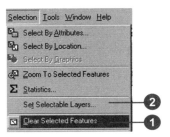

2. Click Selection and click Set Selectable Layers.

3. Uncheck Hydrants; check Distribution mains, Water laterals, and Water distribution network fittings; then close the dialog box.

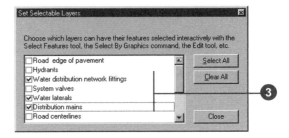

4. Click the Task dropdown arrow and click Create New Feature.

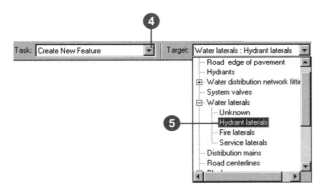

5. Click the Target dropdown arrow. You will see a list of the layers in this database. The Water laterals layer has a plus sign next to it. The plus sign indicates that this layer has subtypes. Click the plus sign and click Hydrant laterals.

The new feature will be created in the Water laterals feature class and will be assigned the Hydrant Lateral subtype.

To establish network connectivity when you add your new hydrant lateral, you must snap it precisely to the distribution main.

6. Click Editor and click Snapping.

The Snapping Environment window appears. When you add the hydrant lateral, you want it to connect to a distribution main.

7. Check the Edge check box next to Distribution mains and uncheck any other boxes that may still be checked. Close the Snapping Environment window.

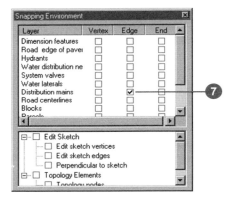

8. Click the Sketch tool.

9. Move the pointer over one of the distribution mains. The pointer snaps to the edge of the distribution main.

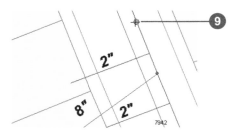

10. With the pointer snapped to the main, click once to start the new hydrant lateral.

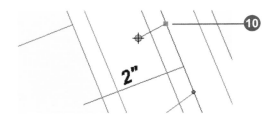

You have just started an *edit sketch*. You create an edit sketch of the geometry when you use the editor tools to create a new feature. After you finish the sketch, the new geometry becomes a feature. You can choose to save or discard your edits when you stop editing.

You will constrain the hydrant lateral to be perpendicular to the distribution main.

11. Move the pointer over the distribution main just south of where you attached the lateral, right-click, and click Perpendicular.

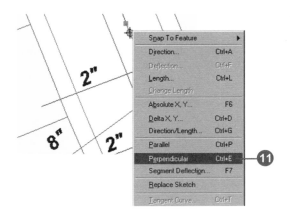

As you move the pointer, you can see that your sketch of the hydrant lateral is constrained to be perpendicular to the distribution main.

Many of the editing tools and commands have keyboard shortcuts associated with them to make editing quicker. You can see the keyboard shortcuts next to the command names in the Edit context menu and on some of the tool windows.

You will now make the lateral 65 feet long.

12. Drag the sketch line to the southwest, then press Ctrl+L. Type "65" and press Enter.

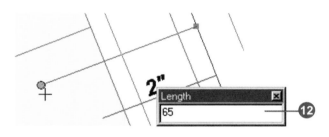

A new vertex is added to the lateral, perpendicular to the distribution main and 65 feet away.

13. Right-click and click Finish Sketch to finish the edit sketch and create the new hydrant lateral.

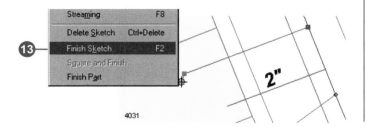

When the new hydrant lateral is created, a number of things happen.

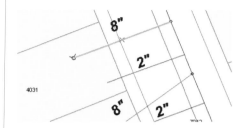

First, a junction between the distribution main and the hydrant lateral is created, and they are topologically connected in the network. The network was created with a *connectivity rule* between these feature types that specifies a default junction, so the new junction is the default junction—in this case, a tap feature.

Next, a junction feature is also added to the other end of the new hydrant lateral. Another connectivity rule exists between water laterals and hydrants. For this rule hydrants were the default junction, so the new junction feature at the southwest end of the lateral is a hydrant.

In addition, when the new hydrant lateral was added, its annotation was also added. A relationship class in the geodatabase links laterals to the LateralDiam annotation feature class. The annotation feature class was created with an advanced labeling expression that labels features longer than 200 feet with their diameter and material type. Since this lateral is less than 200 feet in length and the default value for diameter is 8 inches, the annotation text is 8".

Modifying the hydrant lateral

You'll now modify the hydrant lateral to explore some more geometric network and geodatabase behaviors.

1. Click the Edit tool.

2. Click the lateral and drag it away from the distribution main, then release the mouse button to drop the lateral.

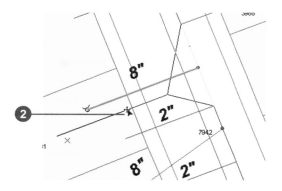

The distribution main stretches to stay connected with the lateral. The distribution main feature is a complex edge feature—it is split in the *logical network* by the addition of the lateral, but it remains a single feature in the geometric network. The annotation also moves with the feature.

3. Click the Undo button to undo the move.

Now you will change the value for the diameter of the lateral.

4. Click the Attributes button.

The new hydrant lateral's attributes are displayed. Some of the fields already have default values that were defined in the geodatabase for this subtype of Water laterals, while other fields have null values.

5. Click the DIAMETER value.

6. Click the dropdown arrow and click 6".

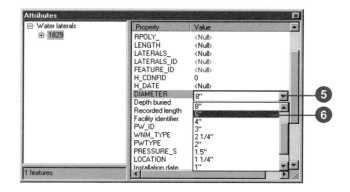

This geodatabase has a coded value domain of valid pipe diameters. The diameter field for hydrant laterals references this diameter value domain. Several different feature classes or subtypes can reference the same coded value domain.

Since the annotation for laterals is derived in part from the value of the DIAMETER field, when you clicked the new value for the diameter, the annotation was automatically updated to reflect the change.

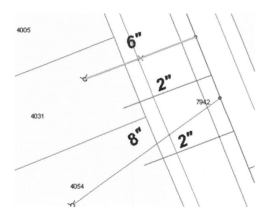

7. Close the Attributes dialog box.

Creating a new dimension feature

The water department wants the geodatabase to show how far the hydrant you added is from the one you moved. You will create a new dimension feature to display this distance. You will create this new dimension feature using the Dimensions feature class in your geodatabase.

1. Click Editor, point to More Editing Tools, and click Dimensioning.

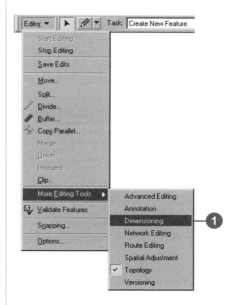

The Dimensioning toolbar lets you choose dimensioning construction methods and styles for your new dimension features.

2. Click the Target layer dropdown arrow on the Editor toolbar and click Dimension features.

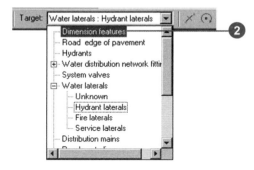

The Dimensioning toolbar becomes active.

You will use the Aligned construction method to construct an aligned dimension feature. This is the default construction method, though there are several others available. Since you are dimensioning features in your water network, you will use the Water dimensions style.

3. Click the Style dropdown arrow; the dimension styles in the Dimensions feature class are listed. Click the Water dimensions style.

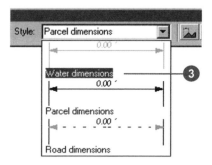

4. Click the Editor menu and click Snapping.

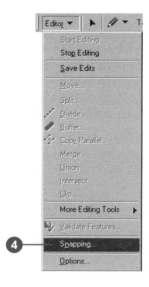

The Snapping Environment window appears. Since you are creating a dimension feature to display the length between two hydrants, you need to set your snapping to the vertices of hydrants.

5. Check Vertex next to Hydrants.

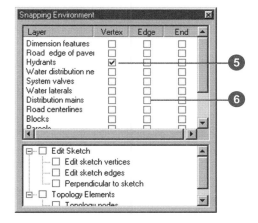

6. Uncheck Edge next to Distribution mains, then close the Snapping Environment window.

7. Click the Sketch tool.

8. Move the pointer over one of the hydrants. The pointer snaps to the hydrant.

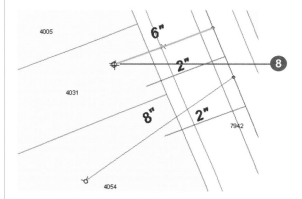

9. With the pointer snapped to the hydrant, click once to start an edit sketch.

10. Move the pointer over the other hydrant.

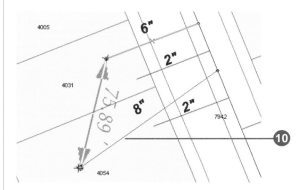

As you move the pointer, the edit sketch draws a preview of the first part of the dimension feature and updates its length.

11. With the pointer snapped to the second hydrant, click once.

12. Move the pointer away from the hydrant.

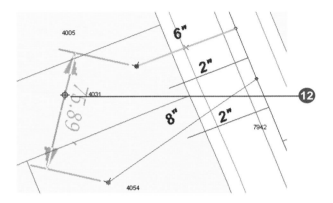

As you move the pointer, the dimension feature's height changes.

13. When you have dragged the dimension feature to the height you want, click once.

Since you are using the Aligned construction method, the sketch is automatically finished after the three points are input and your dimension feature is finished. You can save your edits and your map document if you want.

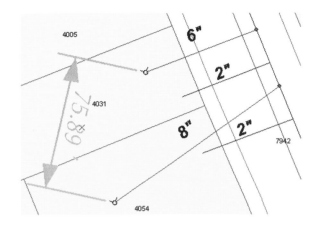

In this quick-start tutorial, you have used ArcMap to take advantage of advanced geodatabase capabilities, including topology, geometric networks, relationship classes, feature subtypes, attribute domains, default values, feature-linked annotation, and dimension features.

The next section of this workbook contains exercises to help you learn how to use ArcMap to edit features. The last section of the book contains exercises to help you learn how to construct a geodatabase with the advanced capabilities you've worked with in this quick-start tutorial.

Editing GIS features

3

IN THIS CHAPTER

- **Exercise 1: Creating polygon features**

- **Exercise 2: Creating line features**

- **Exercise 3: Using a digitizing tablet**

- **Exercise 4: Editing features**

- **Exercise 5: Editing adjacent features with a map topology**

- **Exercise 6: Importing CAD features**

- **Exercise 7: Using geodatabase topology to clean up your data**

- **Exercise 8: Using the Spatial Adjustment tool**

- **Exercise 9: Using the Attribute Transfer tool**

- **Exercise 10: Creating and editing annotation**

ArcMap has the tools you need to create and edit your spatial data. With ArcMap you can create and edit features in shapefiles or a geodatabase. ArcView licensed seats of ArcMap allow you to create a temporary map topology so you can simultaneously edit features that share geometry across multiple feature classes. With ArcEditor or ArcInfo licensed seats of ArcMap, you also have access to advanced editing tools, geometric network editing, and geodatabase topology editing and management.

The easiest way to learn how to edit in ArcMap is to complete the exercises in this tutorial. Most of these tutorials can be completed with ArcView seats of ArcMap—the exceptions are the geodatabase topology exercises.

Exercises 1 and 2 introduce the edit sketch, sketch tools, and edit tasks and show you how to use them to create new features quickly and easily.

Exercise 3 walks you through the process of converting features on a paper map directly into your database using a digitizing tablet.

Exercise 4 teaches you how to move, rotate, scale, extend, trim, and modify the vertices of existing features.

Exercise 5 shows you how to create and maintain the shared boundaries between features and layers with a map topology.

Exercise 6 demonstrates how you can integrate layers from CAD drawings into your database.

Exercise 7 shows you how to clean up existing data and create new features that share boundaries between features and layers with a geodatabase topology.

Exercise 8 shows you how to use the Spatial Adjustment tool to transform, rubbersheet, and edgematch your data.

Exercise 9 teaches you how to use the Attribute Transfer tool to transfer the attributes from one feature to another.

Exercise 10 teaches you how to convert labels to annotation in a geodatabase, place unplaced annotation features, and edit annotation features.

Each of these exercises takes between 15 and 20 minutes to complete. You have the option of working through the entire tutorial or completing each exercise one at a time.

Exercise 1: Creating polygon features

The editing tools in ArcMap make it easy to create new features. You use edit tasks, the edit sketch, sketch tools, and snapping to create new features in ArcMap.

In this exercise, you will digitize a new polygon feature into a shapefile layer that outlines a land use study region. The study area polygon that you create needs to snap to an index grid layer that subdivides the entire geographic region. You will begin by starting ArcMap and loading a map document that contains the shapefile layer and a geodatabase that contains the index grid for the region.

Starting ArcMap and beginning editing

Before you can complete the tasks in this tutorial, you must start ArcMap and load the tutorial data.

1. Double-click a shortcut installed on your desktop or use the Programs list in your Start menu to start ArcMap.

2. Click the Open button on the Standard toolbar. Navigate to the CreatingNewFeatures.mxd map document in the Editor directory where you installed the tutorial data (C:\ArcGIS\ArcTutor is the default location). Click the map and click Open.

3. Click the Editor Toolbar button on the Standard toolbar to add the Editor toolbar to ArcMap.

4. Click the Editor menu and click Start Editing.

If you only have one workspace in your map, you can start editing the map layers at this point. In this exercise, two workspaces are loaded in the map, so you will need to choose the workspace you want to edit.

5. Click the Editor folder workspace to start editing the studyarea.shp shapefile. Click OK. You will edit the geodatabase in the next exercise.

Creating a new polygon feature

This exercise focuses on creating a new study area polygon that encompasses a parcel CAD drawing. The extent of the study area is defined by the index grid lines located in an existing database. The index grid represents logical divisions within the data.

To create the new polygon, you must do *heads-up digitizing* against the index grid and snap the vertices of your new polygon to the vertices of the grid lines.

Setting the snapping environment

Before you start editing the study area shapefile, you need to set your snapping environment so each point you add snaps to the vertices of features in the index grid. For more information about snapping, see 'Using the snapping environment' in *Editing in ArcMap*.

1. Click the Editor menu and click Snapping to display the Snapping Environment dialog box.

2. Check the Vertex check box next to the IndexGrid layer to snap the sketch vertices to the vertices of the index grid. Close the Snapping Environment dialog box.

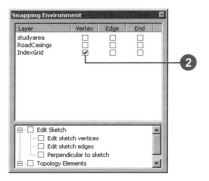

With the snapping environment set, you can create a new study area polygon. Make sure you snap each point to the thick index grid lines shown below.

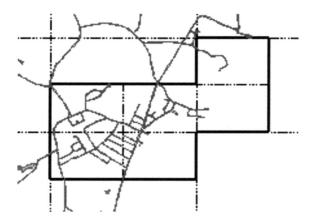

Setting the current task

Before you start digitizing a new feature, you must set the current editing task to Create New Feature.

1. Click the Task dropdown arrow and click Create New Feature.

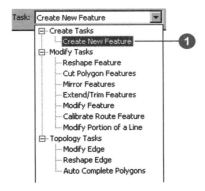

To create a new feature, you also need a target layer. The target layer determines the type of feature you will create and what layer it will be stored in. Since there is only one shapefile in the folder that you started to edit, the target layer is set to the study area shapefile by default.

Using the Sketch tool

To create a new feature using the Create New Feature task, you must first create an edit sketch. An edit sketch is a shape that you draw by digitizing vertices using the sketch construction tools located on the tool palette.

Several tools can add vertices to the sketch. You will use the Sketch tool to add the study area polygon.

1. Click the tool palette dropdown arrow and click the Sketch tool.

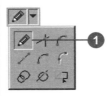

2. Click to add the first vertex of the sketch to the lower left corner of the thick index grid lines. The vertex should snap in place.

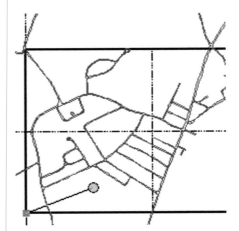

3. Click to add the remaining vertices, snapping each vertex to a corner in the index grid. Create vertices counterclockwise until you return to the point located directly above the first vertex that you placed.

Finishing the sketch

1. Press the F2 key or right-click and click Finish Sketch.

   This action adds the final sketch segment and creates the new feature.

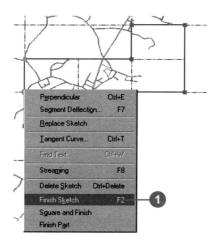

Your new study area polygon is now created. If you snapped each sketch vertex properly, the new polygon should look like the shaded polygon below.

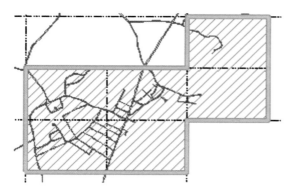

Adding attributes

The new feature you created does not contain any attribute information. Because other polygon features are present in this shapefile, distinguish your new polygon from the others by adding descriptive information about it.

You can add descriptive information for a selected feature using the Attributes dialog box.

1. Click the Attributes button on the Editor toolbar to add a description attribute to the new study area polygon.

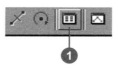

2. Click the layer field for the selected feature and type "StudyArea" as a description of the feature.

Saving your edits

After you have created the new study area polygon, you can choose to save or discard your edits by stopping the edit session.

1. Click the Editor menu and click Stop Editing.

2. Click Yes to save the new study area polygon into the study area shapefile you were editing or No to discard your edits.

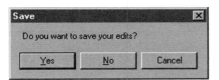

In this exercise you learned how to quickly and accurately create a new polygon feature. You used the Sketch tool to digitize a polygon shape while snapping each vertex to an existing vertex in another layer.

There are several other ways that you can construct new features in your GIS database. The next exercise will show you some of the more advanced methods of constructing vertices in the edit sketch.

For more detailed information about editing tasks and creating polygon features, see the 'Creating new features' chapter in *Editing in ArcMap*.

Exercise 2: Creating line features

In this exercise, you will update your database with a new road casing line.

In building the line feature, you will learn how to use some of the more advanced construction methods offered with the Sketch tool context menu.

Editing the geodatabase

Because the road feature class exists inside a different workspace than the study area shapefile, you need to start editing the database before you can create the new line.

1. Click the Editor menu and click Start Editing. Choose the personal geodatabase as the workspace that you want to edit and click OK.

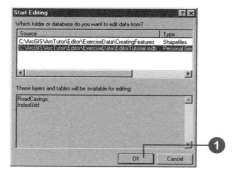

Locating the update area

Spatial bookmarks are named extents that can be saved in map documents. Creating a bookmark for areas that you visit frequently will save you time. For information on how to create and manage spatial bookmarks, see the 'ArcMap basics' chapter in *Using ArcMap*.

You will now zoom to a spatial bookmark created for this exercise.

1. Click the View menu, point to Bookmarks, then click Update road casings to set the current view to the edit area of this exercise.

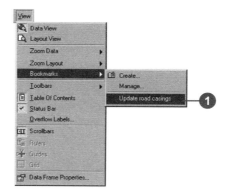

When the display refreshes, note that the top line of this road casing is missing from the layer. You must update the road casing by adding the missing line.

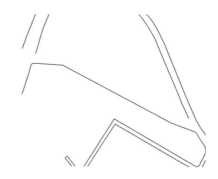

Setting the snapping environment

The endpoints of the road casing feature need to snap to adjacent casings to ensure that the new feature is connected to the existing casing features. Snapping to the end of road casing lines will help you do this.

1. Click the Editor menu and click Snapping. Check the End option for the RoadCasings layer to set snapping to the endpoint of casing features. Uncheck any other boxes that may still be checked and close the dialog box.

Digitizing

After setting the snapping environment, make sure the target layer is set to the RoadCasings layer. Now you can start digitizing.

1. Click the tool palette dropdown arrow and click the Sketch tool.

2. Move the pointer to the broken section of the road casing in the top left corner of the canvas. Once the

pointer is inside the snapping tolerance, the snapping location (blue dot) will jump to the vertex. Click the left mouse button to add the first vertex.

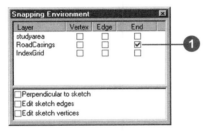

Beginning construction

With the first vertex of the new road casing properly placed, you can construct the casing line feature. Your new feature will be connected to that casing.

Setting length and angle measurements

Before creating the second vertex, you must first set the length of the line.

1. Right-click the map and click Length.

2. Type a value of 15 map units and press Enter.

If you move the pointer now, notice that you can't stretch the line further than your length measurement. This is called a *constraint*. To learn more about sketch constraints, see the chapter 'Creating new features' in *Editing in ArcMap*.

You must also set an angle constraint to create the second vertex.

3. Press Ctrl+A and type a value of "260" degrees. Press Enter.

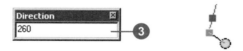

Creating a curve tangent to the last segment

You will add a curve that is tangent to the last segment you added to the sketch. The curve will form the corner of the road casing.

1. Right-click and click Tangent Curve to enter the curve information required to place the next vertex.

2. Click the first dropdown arrow and click Chord. Type "20" to set the chord length. Click the second dropdown arrow and click Delta Angle. Type "90" in the second text box for the angle measurement. Click Left to indicate that the new curve will be tangent to the left of the previous segment. Press Enter to create the curve.

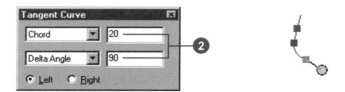

Creating a vertex relative to the last vertex

Often, construction points are calculated relative to the last point recorded. Using the Delta X, Y sketch constructor, you can add relative vertices.

1. Press Ctrl+D. Type "88" for the x-value and "-9" for the y-value. Press Enter to add the point.

Creating a vertex parallel to an existing line

You can define the angle measurement for points added to the sketch in several ways. You can set an absolute value like you did in the first step of this exercise, or you can use the angles of existing features. Quite often, road casings are constructed using the angles of road centerlines. Since you already have one road casing, you can use its angle in constructing the next segment.

1. Right-click the lower road casing line. Click Parallel. Press Ctrl+L, type a value of "415", then press Enter.

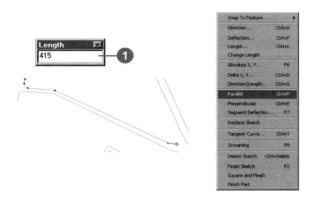

Creating a new vertex using absolute coordinates

Exact x and y coordinate information is often available for the construction of vertices. Add the next vertex by typing exact coordinates using the Absolute X, Y constructor.

1. Right-click on the map and click Absolute X, Y. Type "1227820.6" in the x field, press the Tab key, and type "181460.6" in the y field. Press Enter to add the point.

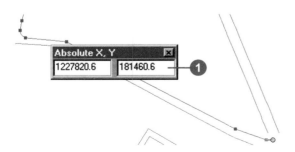

Creating a tangent curve

One final tangent curve needs to be added to the sketch before you can connect it to the existing casing and add the feature.

1. Press Ctrl+T. Type a chord length of 12 and a delta angle of 120, then press Enter to create the final curve segment.

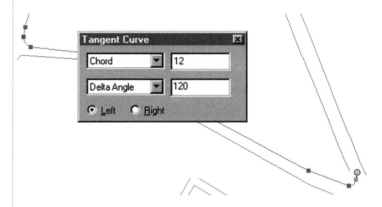

Finishing the sketch

To finish the sketch and create the feature so it is connected to the existing casing, you need to snap the last point of the sketch to the endpoint of the existing road casing.

1. Move the pointer to the endpoint of the existing road casing until it snaps. Double-click to add the last point and create the feature.

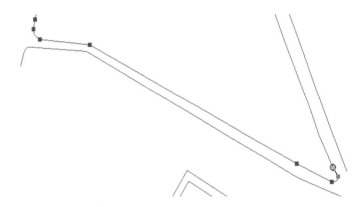

With construction now complete, you can continue to search the layer to find additional broken lines and connect them together, experimenting with these and other sketch tools and construction techniques. You can save your edits and the map document if you want.

The next exercise will show you how you can use the construction methods demonstrated in this exercise to capture features from a paper map directly into your GIS layers using a digitizing tablet.

Exercise 3: Using a digitizing tablet

The first exercise in this chapter showed you how to heads-up digitize features by snapping to an existing vector source. However, often that source information is in paper form. ArcMap lets you trace over the features you are interested in capturing using a digitizing tablet connected to your computer. By *digitizing* data using a tablet, you can get features from almost any paper map into your GIS database.

Setting up your digitizing tablet

Before you can start digitizing, you must set up your tablet and prepare the map from which you want to digitize features. To use a digitizing tablet with ArcMap, it must have WinTab™-compliant digitizer driver software. To find out if a WinTab-compliant driver is available for your digitizer, see the documentation that came with the tablet or contact the manufacturer.

After installing the driver software, use the WinTab manager setup program to configure the buttons on your digitizer puck. One puck button should be configured to perform a left mouse click to digitize point features and vertices; another button should be configured to perform a left double-click to finish digitizing line or polygon features. You may also want to configure a button to perform a right-click so you can access context menus.

If you installed ArcMap before installing your digitizer, the Digitizer tab may not appear in the Editing Options dialog box. To add the tab, you must register the ArcMap digitizer.dll file. To learn how to register digitizer.dll and to find more information on digitizing, see the 'Using a digitizer' chapter in *Editing in ArcMap*.

Preparing the map

You will now print the paper map from which you want to digitize and attach it to your tablet.

1. Print the DigitizingFeatures.tif image located in the Editor tutorial directory where you installed the tutorial data. The default installation path is C:\ArcGIS\ArcTutor\Editor\ExerciseData\Digitizing.

2. Attach the paper map to your digitizing tablet using masking tape, drafting tape, or a special residue-free putty. Drafting tape looks like masking tape, but leaves less residue when it's removed.

3. Start ArcMap if you haven't already done so.

4. Open the DigitizingFeatures.mxd map document so you can register the paper map to your map document.

Registering your map for the first time

You must always register your paper map before you can begin digitizing from it. This involves establishing control points to register the paper map to the geographic space of your GIS data. If your map has a grid or a set of known ground points, you can use these as your control points. If not, choose four to 10 distinctive locations and mark them on your map with a pencil. Give each location a unique number and write down its actual ground coordinates. Control points can also be saved to and loaded from x,y coordinates stored in a comma-delimited text file.

In this exercise, the control points and their ground coordinates are identified for you on the paper map.

1. Click Editor and click Start Editing.

2. Click Editor and click Options.

3. Click the Digitizer tab. You will create and store control points here. The control points you add will be saved with the map document.

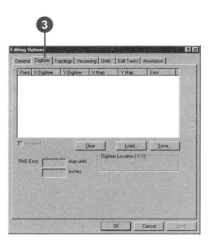

4. In the upper left corner of your paper map, locate the point marked Control Pt.1 and click it using the digitizer puck.

   A record appears in the X Digitizer and Y Digitizer columns for the control point you digitized.

5. Type the actual ground x,y coordinates (labeled X = 711907 and Y = 943420 on the paper map) in the X Map and Y Map fields.

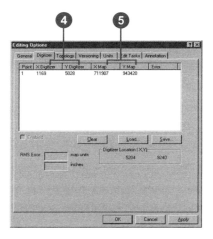

6. Working clockwise, click each of the three other control points on your paper map. After each control point you digitize, type the actual ground coordinates in the X Map and Y Map fields.

   An error in map units is displayed for each control point.

7. After you have digitized all the control points and typed their actual ground coordinates, the total root mean square (RMS) error is calculated and displayed in map and digitizer units. Your X and Y Digitizer and error values may be different from the ones in this example.

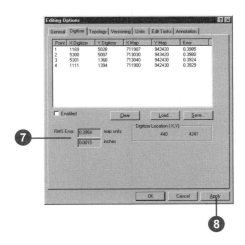

To maintain highly accurate data, your RMS error should be less than 0.004 digitizer units (often inches) or the equivalent scaled distance in *map units*—the ground units in which the coordinates are stored. The map units for this dataset are meters. You can see what the map units are and set the onscreen *display units* by clicking View, Data Frame Properties, then the General tab on the Data Frame Properties dialog box.

You can redigitize control points by selecting the point you want to replace from the list, then clicking your paper map to capture a new control point. Redigitizing points with large error values can help reduce the total RMS error.

8. Click Apply to accept the registration after you have reached an acceptable RMS error.

Digitizing modes

You need to enable *digitizing mode* once you have registered your map. Enabling digitizing mode maps the location of the puck on the tablet to a specific location on the screen.

1. Check the Enabled box on the Digitizer tab of the Editing Options dialog box to enable digitizing mode.

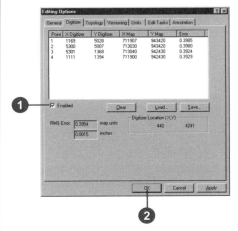

2. Click OK.

Digitizing new features

You are now ready to begin digitizing new features. You will add new lot lines representing a new parcel subdivision into an existing shapefile of lot lines.

To get a better view of the area you'll digitize in, you'll zoom to a spatial bookmark that has been defined for you.

1. Click View, point to Bookmarks, and click Paper Map.

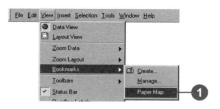

The map zooms to the area of your paper map.

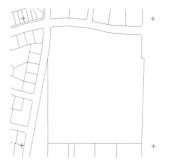

Setting the current task and target layer

Creating new features using a digitizer puck is identical to creating new features using the mouse. You must set the current task and target layer before you start digitizing.

1. Click the Task dropdown arrow and click Create New Feature.

2. Click the Target layer dropdown arrow and click Lotlines to set the target layer.

Creating new features

There are two ways to digitize features: point mode digitizing and stream mode digitizing (streaming). You can toggle between point and stream mode by pressing the F8 key or by right-clicking with the Sketch tool active and clicking Streaming from the menu. Point and stream mode digitizing are available either when you're using a digitizing tablet or when you're digitizing onscreen with your mouse.

Point mode is the default and most common method of digitizing features that are on paper maps. In point mode, you convert a feature on a paper map by digitizing a series of points, or vertices. ArcMap then connects the vertices to create a digital feature. You generally use point mode when precise digitizing is required—for example, when digitizing a perfectly straight line.

Stream mode digitizing provides a quick and easy way to capture features on a paper map when you don't require as much precision or when you're digitizing smooth, curved lines—for example, rivers, streams, and contour lines. With stream mode, you create the first vertex of the feature and trace over the rest of the feature with the digitizer puck. When you're finished tracing, you use the puck to complete the feature.

As you stream, ArcMap automatically adds vertices at an interval you specify; this interval, expressed in current map units, is called the *stream tolerance*. You can change the stream tolerance at any time, even while you're in the process of digitizing a feature.

Digitizing in point mode

1. Click Editor and click Snapping.

2. Check the Edge box for the Lotlines layer so the features you digitize snap to existing edges. Close the Snapping Environment dialog box.

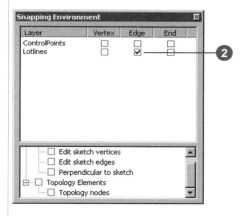

3. Click the Sketch tool.

The lines you are going to digitize now are the exterior boundary lot lines. These lines are drawn in blue.

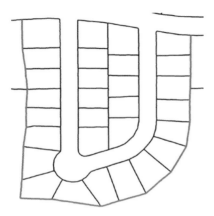

4. Using the puck, click the upper leftmost point of the exterior boundary lot line to start digitizing. You'll notice that the cursor snaps to the edges of the lot lines.

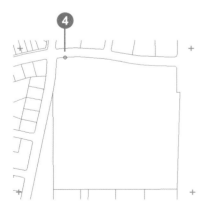

For straight segments, you should add a vertex where lot lines intersect. In curved segments, you should click more points to make sure their shapes are defined.

5. When you're done with your sketch, finish it by clicking the button on your puck that you configured as a double-click.

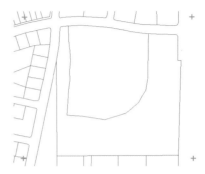

Digitizing in stream mode

When tracing line or polygon features, you may want to add vertices as you move the mouse rather than clicking each time you want to add a vertex. Stream mode digitizing lets you do this.

Before starting to digitize in stream mode, you need to set a stream tolerance—the interval at which the sketch adds vertices along the feature you are digitizing. The default tolerance value is 0 map units, so if you don't enter a tolerance value, you may find vertices that overlap each other.

You will also specify the group tolerance—the number of streaming vertices you want to group together. The number you set tells ArcMap how many vertices to delete when you click the Undo button. For example, if you set this number to 20 and click the Undo button while you're digitizing a feature, ArcMap deletes the last 20 digitized vertices from your feature.

You are now going to digitize the frontage lot lines—the lines drawn in red—that define the road leading into the new subdivision. You will digitize these lot lines as two features, one for the outer line and one for the inner line.

Start here to digitize the first line.

Start here to digitize the second line.

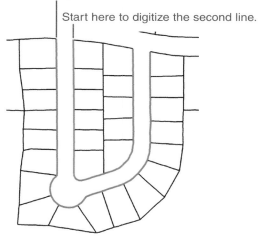

1. Click Editor and click Options.

2. Click the General tab.

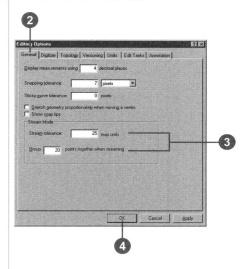

3. Type a stream tolerance value of 25 map units and set the group tolerance to 20.

4. Click OK.

5. Click the Sketch tool.

6. Snap the cursor to the upper leftmost point of the outer frontage lot line, but don't click yet.

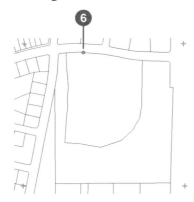

7. Press F8 to start digitizing in stream mode.

8. Click to start the sketch.

9. Carefully trace along the boundary of the lots until you reach the last lot in the upper right. Notice that vertices are added at consistent intervals that are 25 map units apart. Although you're working in stream mode, you can still click when you want to add a point by hand.

   If you make a mistake while streaming, you can click the Undo button to remove the last 20 vertices. You'll need to press F8 to suspend streaming while you're choosing interface elements, and press F8 again when you want to return to stream mode digitizing.

Undo will delete 20 vertices—the number set in the group tolerance—at a time.

10. Snap the last vertex of your line to the existing lot line and finish the sketch by clicking the button on your puck that you configured as a double-click.

Now you are going to digitize the second red line, the inner frontage lot line.

11. Snap the cursor to the existing lot line and click to start digitizing the inner frontage line. You should still be in streaming mode, but if you find yourself in point mode, press F8 to switch to streaming.

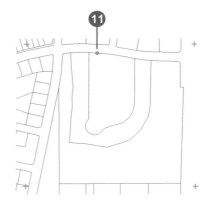

12. Carefully trace along the boundary of the lots until you reach the last lot in the upper rightmost point of the inner frontage line.

13. Snap the cursor to the existing lot line and press F8 to stop digitizing in stream mode.

14. Finish the sketch by clicking the button on your puck that you configured as a double-click.

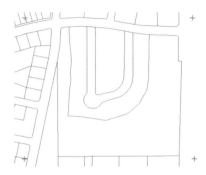

With the exterior boundary lines and the outer and inner frontage lot lines digitized, use point mode to digitize the remaining line features that define the lots.

Once you've digitized all the new lot lines, your map should look like this:

Disabling the puck

After you're finished digitizing, you should disable the digitizer puck.

1. Click Editor and click Options.

2. Click the Digitizer tab and uncheck Enabled to disable the digitizer.

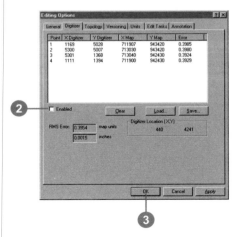

3. Click OK.

Finishing your digitizing session

Once you have finished tracing lot lines and have disabled the digitizer puck, you can stop editing and complete the exercise by saving your edits.

1. Click Editor and click Stop Editing.

2. Click Yes to save your edits.

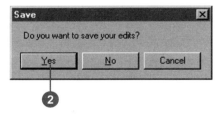

In this exercise you learned how to create new features in your GIS database by digitizing shapes directly from a digitizing tablet. The next exercise will show you how to copy shapes from existing vector sources—CAD drawing layers—and paste them into your GIS database.

To learn more about digitizing, see the 'Using a digitizer' chapter in *Editing in ArcMap* or the ArcGIS Desktop Help. If you need to find out if ArcMap supports your digitizing tablet, consult the ESRI Web site at *www.esri.com* for the most recent information.

Exercise 4: Editing features

In the first three exercises, you learned how to create new features in ArcMap. In this exercise, you'll learn how to copy and paste, move, rotate, scale, and extend existing features.

Opening the exercise document and starting an edit session

1. Start ArcMap.
2. Click the Open button on the Standard toolbar. Navigate to the EditingFeatures.mxd map document located in the Editor directory where you installed the tutorial data (C:\ArcGIS\ArcTutor is the default location).

3. Click the Editor menu and click Start Editing.

Copying and pasting features

When creating vector features of the same type as existing ones, it is more efficient to copy their shapes than to digitize over the top of them. You can copy the shapes of any vector feature that you can select in ArcMap. In this step, you will select buildings from a CAD drawing and paste them into a geodatabase layer of buildings.

1. Click the Edit tool on the Editor toolbar and drag a box around all of the new building features to select them.

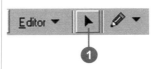

All selected CAD features should be highlighted as shown below.

2. Click the Copy button on the Standard toolbar to copy the selected features to the clipboard.

3. Set the Buildings layer as the target layer so you can paste the copied features into it.

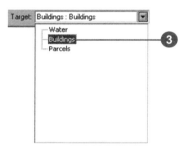

4. Click Paste to copy the selected building features into the target layer. The progress bar will update as each feature is copied into the target layer.

It is important to note that only the shapes are copied from the CAD file into the geodatabase. If you need to paste the attributes as well, you must use the object loader. Exercise 6 of this chapter shows you how to do this.

Rotating features

Now that you've copied the building features into the Buildings layer of your geodatabase, you need to orient the features to fit the parcel subdivision into which you'll move them.

1. To avoid selecting features from the CAD layer—called New Buildings—uncheck it in the table of contents to hide its features.

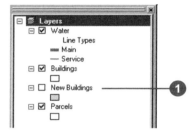

2. Click the Rotate tool on the Editor toolbar.

3. Press the A key, type "180", and press Enter to rotate the selected building features 180 degrees.

The selected features are now oriented 180 degrees from their previous location.

Moving features

Now that the buildings are oriented properly, you are ready to move and scale them so that they fit inside the subdivision located near the bottom center of the map.

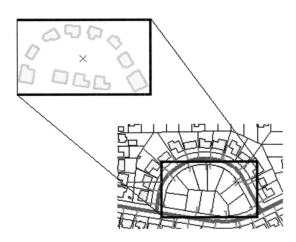

You can ensure the proper relocation of the building features by snapping the lower left selected building feature to the endpoint of the lower left water service line, shown in red.

1. With the buildings selected, click the Editor menu and click Snapping.

2. Check the End option for the Water layer and the Vertex option for the Buildings layer so you can snap the corner of a building feature to the endpoint of a waterline. Close the dialog box.

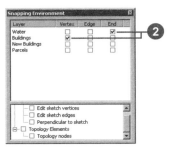

3. Click the Edit tool so you can move the selection anchor for selected features.

The selection anchor is a small x located at the center of selected features. It is the point on the feature or group of features that will be snapped when you move them.

4. Hold down the Ctrl key and move the pointer over the selection anchor. When the pointer icon changes, click and drag the selection anchor until it snaps to the corner of the lower left building.

5. Drag the selected buildings until they snap to the endpoint of the waterline.

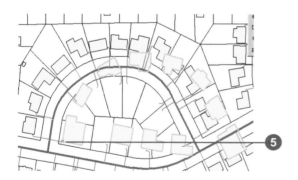

Notice that some of the buildings are too large to fit inside the parcels. You must scale these features to make them fit.

Scaling features

When data is created using a coordinate system different from that of your database, you may need to adjust the projection and scale of the data to fit the projection and scale of your database. Often, simply moving, rotating, and scaling those features are sufficient.

Because scaling is not a common operation, the Scale tool is not located on the Editor toolbar. You must, therefore, add it to the toolbar before you can use it.

1. Click the Tools menu and click Customize.

2. Click the Commands tab and click Editor in the Categories list. The Editor category contains many editing tools, regardless of their location.

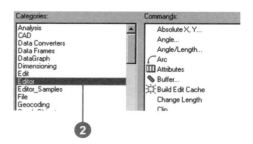

3. Scroll down the list of commands on the right until you find the Scale tool. Drag and drop the tool next to the Rotate tool on the Editor toolbar. Click Close on the Customize dialog box.

4. Before scaling the selected features, you may want to zoom in so that your scaling is more accurate. Click the Selection menu and click Zoom To Selected Features.

5. Click the Scale tool and drag the selected building features to scale them. Shrink the features until they fit inside the parcel subdivisions. Use the waterlines as a guide. Scale features until the lower right building matches the endpoint of the waterline.

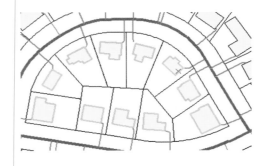

Extending and trimming waterlines using the Extend/Trim Features task

Now that you have scaled the building features to fit inside the parcel subdivision, you need to extend the waterlines so that they snap to the side of each building. You can extend and trim waterlines using the Extend/Trim Features task.

1. To get a better view of the waterline that you need to extend, you can zoom in to the Extend Water Line bookmark. Click the View menu, point to Bookmarks, and click Extend Water Line.

2. Click the Task dropdown arrow and click Extend/Trim Features to set the edit task.

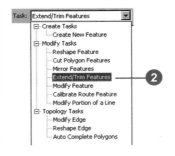

3. The Extend/Trim edit task will extend selected polyline features to the sketch you digitize. Click the Edit tool and click the waterline feature that you need to extend.

4. Click the Sketch tool and snap the first sketch point to the upper right corner of the building feature to which you want to extend the water line feature.

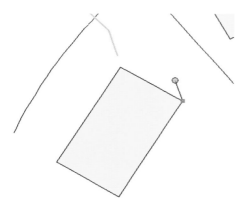

5. Move the pointer until it snaps to the upper left building corner and double-click to finish the sketch. The waterline will then extend until it intersects the line that you have digitized. Since the line is identical to the side of the building, the end of the waterline should snap to the building.

You can also use the Extend/Trim Features task to cut a waterline feature if it extends too far into the building.

6. To get a better view of the waterlines, you must zoom to the bookmarked extent called Trim Water Line, which was created for you. Click the View menu, point to Bookmarks, and click Trim Water Line.

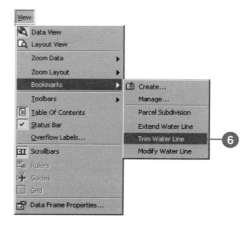

7. Click the Edit tool and click to select the waterline that extends into the building and needs to be trimmed.

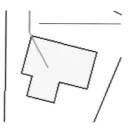

8. If you changed the current task, make sure that you change it back to Extend/Trim Features, then click the Sketch tool to start digitizing.

9. Snap the first sketch point to the lower left corner of the building feature.

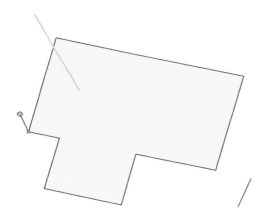

10. Move the pointer to the upper left corner of the building. Double-click to snap the last point of the sketch to the building corner and trim the waterline feature.

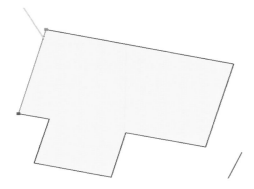

Extending and trimming waterlines using the Modify Features task

The Extend/Trim Features task lets you extend and trim selected waterlines using a sketch that the features either cross or extend to. However, that is not the only method for extending or trimming waterlines. You can move, insert, or remove vertices of the waterline by making its shape the edit sketch. You can do this using the Modify Features task.

1. To get a better view of the waterlines, you need to zoom to the bookmarked extent called Modify Water Line. Click the View menu, point to Bookmarks, and click Modify Water Line.

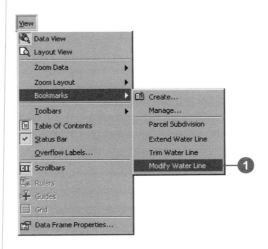

2. Click the Edit tool and click to select the waterline feature that needs to be extended.

3. Click the Task dropdown arrow and click Modify Feature to display the vertices of the waterline.

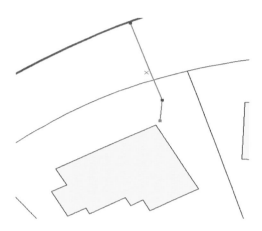

4. Click the Edit tool and move the pointer over the red vertex at the end of the waterline. Drag the vertex until it snaps to the building corner.

5. Move the pointer over the red vertex, right-click, then click Finish Sketch to finish modifying the waterline.

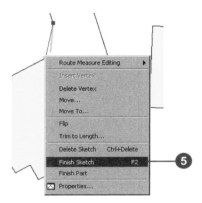

You can follow the same steps to trim line features using the Modify Features task. You can use the Trim command to reduce the length of the sketch by an exact distance as well.

With modifications to these waterlines completed, continue modifying the rest of the waterlines that don't connect to building features and experiment with other methods of modifying shapes.

For more information about editing features, see the 'Editing existing features' chapter in *Editing in ArcMap*.

Exercise 5: Editing adjacent features with a map topology

Many vector datasets contain features that share geometry. Features can share edges—for example, line segments—or nodes, the points at the ends of segments. For example, watershed polygons might have common edges along ridgelines, and lake polygons might share their shoreline edges with land cover polygons. Three watersheds might share a single node at a mountain peak, and three river-reach features might share a node at a confluence. You can simultaneously edit shared edges and nodes with the Topology Edit tool when you create a map topology.

Opening the exercise document

In this exercise you will update multiple watershed features in two feature classes using the Topology Edit tool.

1. Start ArcMap.

2. Click the Open button on the Standard toolbar. Navigate to the MapTopology.mxd map document located in the Editor directory where you installed the tutorial data. (C:\ArcGIS\ArcTutor is the default location.) Click the map and click Open.

This map contains two feature classes. Hydro_region contains polygon features representing three large hydrologic regions in the southwestern United States. Note that part of the Great Basin regional watershed has been omitted from the tutorial dataset. Hydro_units contains polygon features representing smaller watersheds within these regions. You can see the features in the Hydro_units feature class because the Hydro_region features are partly transparent.

The regional data was derived by dissolving the smaller hydrologic units, so the boundaries of the features in Hydro_regions are already coincident with the boundaries of the smaller watersheds. In this exercise you will create a map topology to allow you to edit the vertices that make up a shared edge and move a node that defines the intersection of multiple features.

3. Click Editor and click Start Editing.

   If the Topology toolbar is not on the map, you will add it.

4. Click Editor, point to More Editing Tools, and click Topology.

The Topology toolbar contains tools for working with topologically related features. Some features are related by a topology stored in a geodatabase. With an ArcInfo or ArcEditor license, you can use the topology editing tools on this toolbar to edit such geodatabase topologies. For more information on editing geodatabase topology, see the 'Using a geodatabase topology' exercise and the 'Editing topology' chapter of *Editing in ArcMap*.

You may still need to edit features that share geometry when you are working with shapefiles or features in a geodatabase that do not have a topology defined for them. You can use the tools on this toolbar to create a temporary topological relationship between coincident parts of features—a map topology—then edit the shared parts of features. ArcView licensed seats of ArcMap can edit map topologies but not geodatabase topologies. ArcEditor and ArcInfo licensed seats of ArcMap can edit both types of topology.

Creating a map topology for an area

Before you create the map topology, you'll zoom in to the area that you want to edit. Zooming in to an area reduces the number of features that the map topology analyzes when building the topology cache.

1. Click View, point to Bookmarks, and click 3 Region Divide.

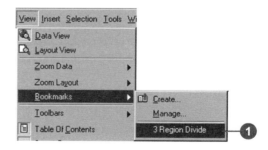

The map zooms to the bookmarked area. Now you can see labels for the smaller watersheds.

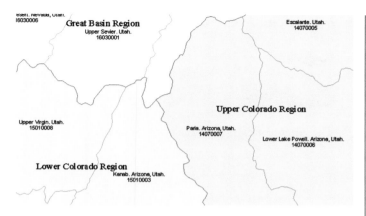

2. Click the Map Topology button.

The Map Topology dialog box appears. You can select the feature classes that will participate in the topology and choose a cluster tolerance. The cluster tolerance defines how close together parts of features must be before they are considered to be coincident.

3. Click Select All.

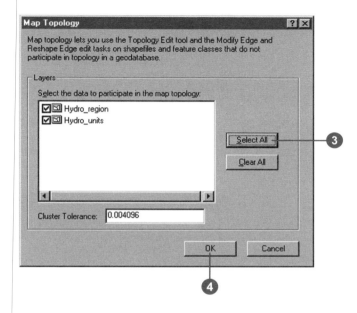

You want all of the features on the map from both feature classes to participate in the map topology.

The default cluster tolerance is the minimum possible cluster tolerance and is given in coordinate system units. In this case the dataset is in the Universal Transverse Mercator coordinate system, and the units are meters. You will accept the default cluster tolerance.

4. Click OK.

Now you will start editing the map topology using the Topology Edit tool.

5. Click the Topology Edit tool.

6. Click the edge that is shared by the East Fork Sevier. Utah, polygon (#16030002) and Kanab. Arizona, Utah, polygon (#15010003).

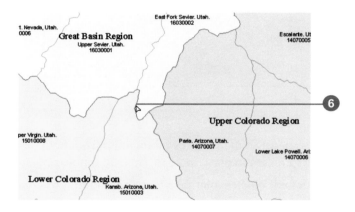

The edge is selected and changes color. If you set ArcMap to show unselected topology nodes while doing the quick-start tutorial, then open circles will also appear around the intersections of the lines that make up the polygon edges. These are unselected nodes in the map topology.

This edge is also shared by the larger regional polygons. To check this you'll use the Show Shared Features tool.

7. Click the Show Shared Features button.

The Shared Features dialog box appears.

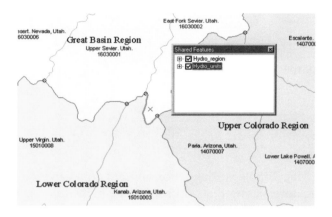

You can use this dialog box to investigate which features share a given topology edge or node. You can also use this dialog box to control whether or not edits that you make to a given topology element will be shared by certain features.

The names of both feature classes in the map topology, Hydro_region and Hydro_units, are listed with check marks in this dialog box. The checks mean that the selected topology element is shared by features in these feature classes. Next, you'll see which features share this edge.

8. Double-click Hydro_units.

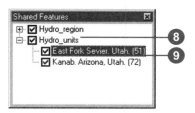

The plus sign changes to a minus, and two more branches expand below Hydro_units. Each of these represents a hydrologic unit feature that shares this edge.

9. Click East Fork Sevier. Utah. (51).

Feature number 51 in the Hydro_units feature class, the East Fork Sevier hydrologic unit, flashes on the map.

10. Double-click Hydro_region and click Great Basin Region (1).

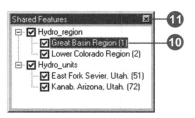

Feature number 1 in the Hydro_region feature class, the Great Basin region, flashes on the map.

11. Close the Shared Features dialog box.

Editing a shared edge in a map topology

Now that you've seen that the features you need to update share this edge, you'll update the boundary of the watersheds to better fit the terrain.

1. Check Hillshaded_terrain.sid to turn on the image in the ArcMap table of contents.

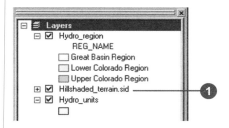

This is a small area of hillshaded terrain extracted from the National Elevation Dataset Shaded Relief Image Service, published by the U.S. Geological Survey. You can add the original image to ArcMap from the Geography Network[SM].

You will use this image, and the guidelines that have been added to it, to update your watershed data.

2. Press and hold the Z key.

   The pointer becomes the Zoom In tool.

3. While pressing the Z key, click and drag a box around the selected edge.

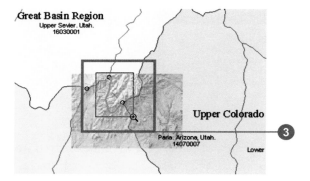

The watershed data that you have is derived from the medium resolution National Hydrography Dataset, published by the United States Geological Survey and the United States Environmental Protection Agency. This data was compiled at a scale of 1:100,000. The National Elevation Dataset hillshade is derived from 1:24,000-scale digital elevation model data. You will use the higher resolution hillshade data to improve the watershed boundaries.

4. Double-click the edge to see the vertices that define the shape of the edge.

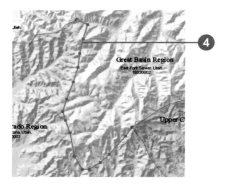

Now you can see the vertices (in green) that define the shape of this edge.

5. Move the pointer over the second vertex from the eastern end of the edge. When the pointer changes to a box with four arrows, click the vertex, drag it northwest, then drop it on the blue guideline.

You could continue reshaping this edge vertex by vertex, but there is a faster way to update it.

6. Click and drag a box across part of the selected edge.

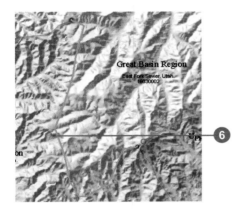

This reselects the edge and refreshes the change you made to it.

Reshape a shared edge in a map topology

Now you'll use an edit sketch to reshape the shared edge. You'll need to set the edit task to Reshape Edge and turn on snapping to the watershed edges.

1. Click the Task dropdown list and click the Reshape Edge topology task.

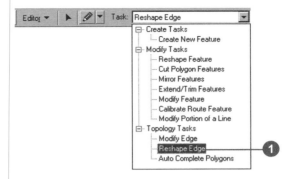

2. Click the Sketch tool on the Editor toolbar.

3. Click Editor and click Snapping.

4. Check the box to snap to edges in the Hydro_region feature class, then close the Snapping Environment dialog box.

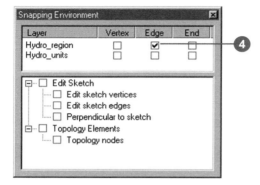

5. Move the pointer over the edge where the selected topology edge and the blue guideline begin to diverge.

6. Click the edge to begin an edit sketch.

7. Continue adding vertices along the guide line.

8. Make sure that the last vertex you add to the sketch snaps to the edge near the vertex you moved.

9. Press F2 or right-click and click Finish Sketch.

The change that you made with the edit sketch is applied to the shared edge.

Move a shared node in a map topology

Now that you've adjusted the edge shared by the watershed boundaries, another problem with the existing data needs to be fixed. The node at the east end of the edge is the point where the Great Basin, Upper Colorado, and Lower Colorado Region watersheds come together. You'll move this shared node by a specified number of meters.

1. Click the Topology Edit tool.

2. Click once on the map, off of the edge, to deselect it.

3. Press and hold the N key.

   This temporarily limits the selectable topology elements to nodes.

4. Click and drag a box around the node while holding the N key.

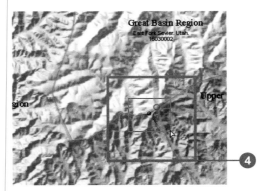

The node is selected. Now you'll move it to the correct location.

5. Right-click and click Move.

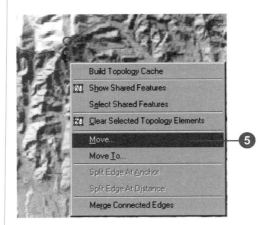

You will move this node 460 meters in the x direction (east) and 410 m in the y direction (north).

6. Type "460" and "410" in the x and y boxes, then press Enter.

The node is moved to the new location, and all of the features that share it in the map topology are updated.

You could also have moved the node by clicking and dragging it, as you moved the vertex of the topology edge.

7. Click Editor and click Stop Editing.

8. Click Yes if you want to save your edits.

In this exercise you learned how to create a map topology and how to use the Topology Edit tool to edit multiple features that share edges and nodes. The map topology allowed you to maintain the common boundary between the features while simultaneously editing four, then six features in two different feature classes. The Topology Edit tool and the topology editing tasks can also be used to edit the edges and nodes in a geodatabase topology.

Exercise 6: Importing CAD features

ArcMap lets you seamlessly integrate computer-aided design drawings into your work. It allows you to display and query CAD datasets without first having to convert the drawing files to an ESRI format.

The ability to work with CAD drawings in ArcMap is particularly useful if your organization has existing CAD data resources that you need to use immediately in your work.

Not only can you perform basic query and analysis functions using ArcMap tools, but you can also snap directly to CAD features or entities when you update your database.

This exercise will show you how to import CAD features directly into your edit session; this will allow you to easily integrate CAD features into your work.

Opening the Exercise document

1. Start ArcMap.
2. Click the Open button on the Standard toolbar. Navigate to the WorkingWithCAD.mxd map document located in the Editor directory where you installed the tutorial data. (C:\ArcGIS\ArcTutor is the default location.)

3. Zoom to the area of the map identified by the red hatched polygon.

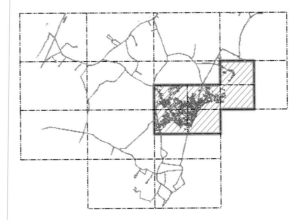

Using the Load Objects wizard

You can import CAD entities directly from CAD feature classes using the Load Objects wizard. However, you'll need to add the Load Objects wizard into ArcMap first.

1. Click the Tools menu and click Customize. Click the Commands tab.

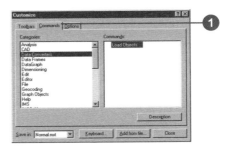

2. Click the Data Converters category from the Categories list and drag and drop the Load Objects command onto the Editor menu. Close the Customize dialog box.

3. Click Editor and click Start Editing. Set the Target layer to the LotLines layer. This is the layer into which you will load the parcel lines.

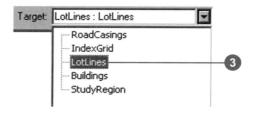

Loading CAD features

With the target layer set to the lot lines feature class, you are ready to load features directly from the CAD drawing.

CAD drawings are represented in two ways: CAD drawing files and CAD drawing datasets. CAD drawing datasets contain feature classes organized by point, line, or polygon shape types.

Each CAD feature in a CAD feature class contains a Layer field; it lets you identify the CAD drawing layer from which each feature is derived. In this exercise, you'll extract the features belonging to the lot line layer of the polyline feature class into your empty lot line geodatabase feature class.

1. Click Editor and click Load Objects.

2. Click the Browse button, located to the right of the Input data list. Navigate to where you installed the ArcTutor sample data (C:\ArcGIS\ArcTutor by default), then navigate to the Editor\ExerciseData\EditingCAD directory.

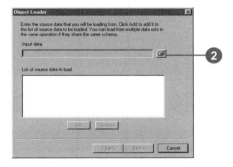

3. Double-click the Parcels.dwg drawing dataset. Click the Polyline feature class and click the Open button.

4. Click the Add button to add the CAD feature class— listed in the Input data list—to the list of source data to load.

5. Click Next.

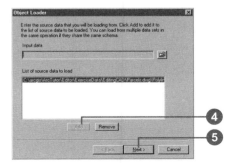

Matching input and target fields

The next step in the wizard lets you match the fields of the CAD feature class with the fields in your target layer.

1. Accept the default field mappings for this exercise. Click Next.

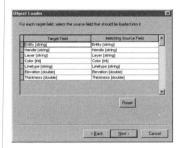

Defining a query

Since all CAD layers are combined into a single feature class containing a Layer attribute value, you will define an attribute query so that only features with a layer name = 'LOT-L' will be loaded into the target layer.

1. Click the option to load only features that satisfy the query.

2. Click Query Builder to define the query.

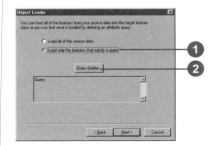

3. Double-click Layer in the Fields list. This adds the string to the where clause for the query.

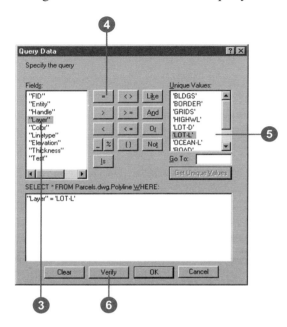

4. Click the equal (=) sign.

5. Click Get Unique Values to display all unique attribute values for the Layer field. Double-click LOT-L from the list to complete the query.

   After completing the steps above, your query should read: "Layer" = 'LOT-L'. You can alter the query by typing directly into the where clause box.

6. Click Verify to ensure that you have created a valid SQL where clause.

7. Click OK. Make sure that you have a valid query expression before applying the query to the wizard.

8. Click Next on the Object Loader dialog box.

Snapping and validation

Next, the Object Loader will ask if you want to apply any snapping agents that you have set in the Snapping Environment dialog box to features as they are loaded into the map and whether you want to validate each feature that is added.

If you're concerned about the connectivity between features that you import and existing features in your database, you may want to apply snapping. However, you should be aware that features will move within the current snapping tolerance. If the source CAD data was constructed using coordinate geometry, applying snapping may reduce the accuracy of the original data.

1. Click Next (do not apply snapping).

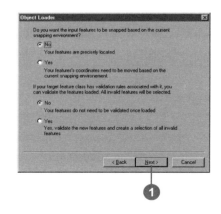

Completing the wizard and loading features

The final dialog box provides a summary of the options that you chose through each step of the wizard. You can examine each of your steps and click Back if you made any mistakes.

1. Click Finish.

   A progress indicator will appear.

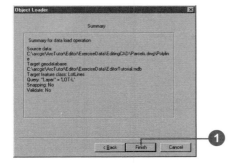

Once the wizard has finished loading features, you may need to refresh the display to see the new lot lines.

Saving your edits

Now that you have successfully loaded CAD data into your edit session, you can stop editing and save your edits.

1. Click Editor and click Stop Editing.

2. Click Yes to save your edits. You'll use this data in the next exercise.

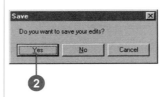

In this exercise, you learned how to load CAD features directly into your GIS database. You were able to import features by their shape type and by their CAD layer name using the Load Objects wizard. But you don't have to import CAD data to use it. You can also snap directly to CAD features or simply display and query their attributes. For more information about CAD drawings, see *Using ArcCatalog*.

Exercise 7: Using geodatabase topology to clean up your data

The CAD lot lines data that you loaded in the previous exercise needs some quality checking, editing, and other processing for you to have useful parcel polygon features for your geodatabase.

You will create a simple geodatabase topology rule to help you find digitizing errors in the lot line data, then use the topology and editing tools to fix these errors. Once the problems, mostly lines that do not close to form polygons, are fixed, you will create a new polygon feature class from the lot lines. You'll add the polygons to the topology, then use the topology to identify and resolve other errors in the data.

If you have not loaded the lot lines, a duplicate of this feature dataset with the lot lines already loaded may be found where the tutorial data is installed at: C:\ArcGIS\ArcTutor\Editor\ExerciseData\ TopologyEdits\TopologyTutorial.mdb.

You must close ArcMap before building the topology to release the lock on the database.

1. Close ArcMap. You do not need to save changes to the map.

Navigating to the study area dataset

1. Start ArcCatalog.

2. Click the Connect to Folder button.

3. Navigate to the ExerciseData folder. The default location for this folder is C:\ArcGIS\ArcTutor\Editor.

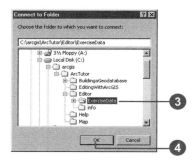

4. Click OK.

5. Double-click the folder connection.

6. Double-click the EditorTutorial.mdb geodatabase.

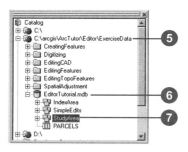

7. Click StudyArea.

This is the feature dataset into which you loaded the CAD lot lines in the previous exercise.

Creating a geodatabase topology

Now you'll create a geodatabase topology to help you find errors in the LotLines data. The topology will be simple, involving one feature class and one topology rule.

1. Right-click the StudyArea dataset, point to New, and click Topology.

2. Click Next.

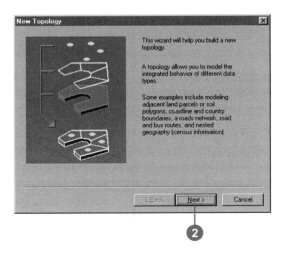

On the next panel of the wizard, you can set the cluster tolerance. The cluster tolerance is the minimum distance that separate parts of features can be from each other. Vertices and edges of features that fall within the cluster tolerance are snapped together.

By default, the wizard gives the smallest possible cluster tolerance, which is determined by the precision of the spatial reference of the dataset. The precision of a dataset defines how many system units can be stored per unit of linear measure and controls how precisely coordinates are stored in the dataset.

This dataset has a precision of about 62,500 units per meter, so the smallest resolvable ground distance in the data is 0.000016 m, or about 1/100th of a millimeter. The actual precision at which the data was collected is considerably coarser.

The cluster tolerance is 0.000033 m. Parts of features within this distance of one another will be snapped together. You'll accept the default cluster tolerance.

3. Click Next.

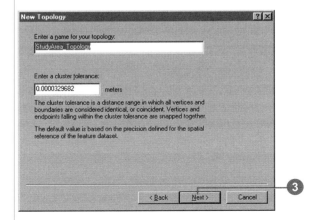

Now you can choose which feature classes in the dataset to include in the topology.

4. Check LotLines.

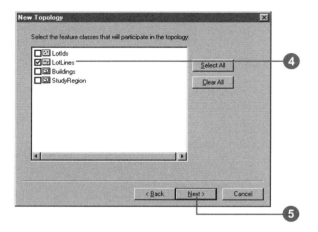

5. Click Next.

When you have more than one feature class in a topology, you can give them different ranks. When vertices or edges of features fall within the cluster tolerance of each other, the feature class ranks control which is moved to the other's location. Feature classes of a lower rank will be snapped to feature classes of a higher rank. The highest rank is 1; the lowest is 50. Parts of features of the same rank that fall within the cluster tolerance are geometrically averaged.

6. Click Next.

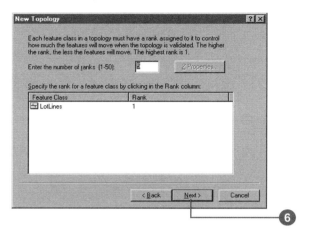

When you build a topology, you can pick the rules that will govern the allowable spatial relationships between features.

7. Click Add Rule.

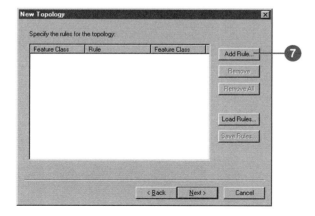

8. Click the Rule dropdown list and click Must Not Have Dangles.

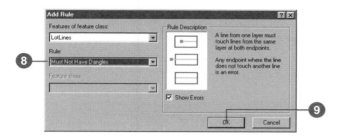

Dangles are the endpoints of lines that are not snapped to other lines in the feature class. You will want to find the dangles in the LotLines feature class because they represent places where the imported CAD line work will not produce closed polygons.

9. Click OK.

The rule is added to the list of topology rules.

10. Click Next.

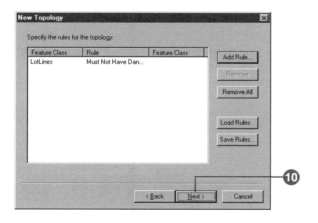

11. Click Finish.

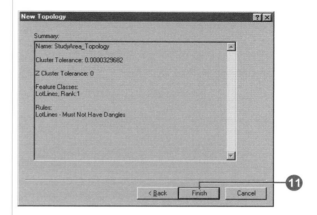

You get a message that the topology is being built, then another asking whether you want to validate the topology now.

12. Click Yes.

You get a message that the topology is being validated, and the new topology appears in the StudyArea dataset.

Adding the topology to the map

Now you'll use the topology to help you find the dangle errors in the LotLines data. It is important to clean up this data before you create polygon features because only one lot polygon will be created if a line dividing two lots does not completely separate them.

1. Click the Launch ArcMap button to start a new map.

2. If the Startup dialog box appears, click the button to start a new empty map.

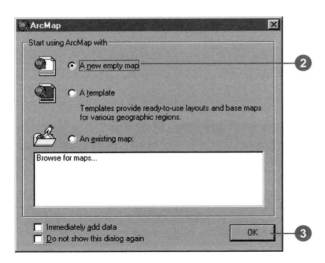

3. Click OK.

4. Resize the ArcMap and ArcCatalog windows so that you can see both.

5. Click StudyArea_Topology and drag it onto the map.

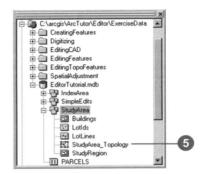

6. Click Yes when you are asked whether to add all of the layers that participate in the topology.

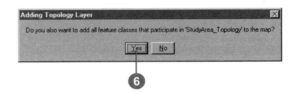

The topology layer and the LotLines features are added to the map.

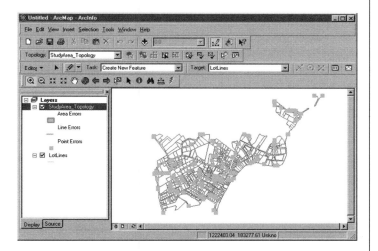

The Topology layer shows all of the topology errors. Notice that in the ArcMap table of contents, the topology layer can show Area, Line, and Point errors. This topology only has one feature class and one rule, so all of the topology errors relate to that rule. The topology rule specifies that LotLines must not have dangles. The error geometry for dangles is a point, located at the dangling end of a line feature. All of the red error features on the map are dangles.

Finding topology errors

The next step to make this data useful is to identify the topology errors that are present. Lot lines that have a dangle, where one end of the line is not connected to another lot line, are errors that you need to find to clean up this data so you can create lot polygons. Some dangles need to be extended to close a polygon; others overshoot the line that they should snap to and need to be trimmed. You will find some of these errors now.

1. Click Editor and click Start Editing.

2. Click the Zoom In tool.

3. Click and drag a box around the three red error features located near the middle of the map, to the right of and above the north–south and east–west trending series of errors.

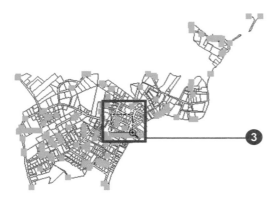

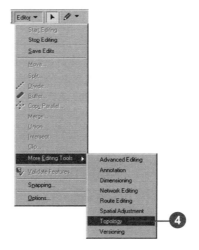

Now you can see three of the errors.

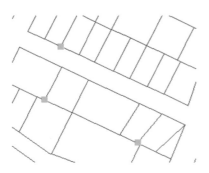

You will use tools on the Topology toolbar to find out more about these errors and to correct them. If the Topology toolbar is visible, skip the next step in which you add the toolbar.

4. Click Editor, point to More Editing Tools, and click Topology.

5. Click the Error Inspector button on the Topology toolbar.

The Error Inspector allows you to manage and interact with all of the topology errors on your map.

6. Check the Errors and Visible Extent only check boxes.

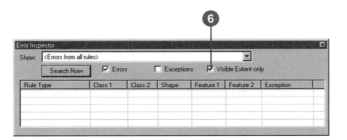

7. Click Search Now.

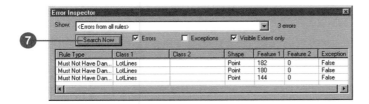

You may see additional errors if the map display changed shape when you added the Error Inspector.

Correcting an overshoot error

All of the errors on the map are violations of the Must Not Have Dangles rule. However, there are several different problems that can cause this type of error. A dangle error can be caused by a line that extends too far beyond the line it is supposed to touch or by a line that doesn't extend quite far enough. These are called overshoots and undershoots, respectively.

Dangles can also occur where features have been digitized from adjacent map sheets. These lines sometimes need to be snapped together so they connect to form a continuous line. Other dangle errors occur at the edge of map sheets, where a line is cut off on the original source data.

You will now correct one of the errors on this map.

1. Click 144 in the Feature 1 column.

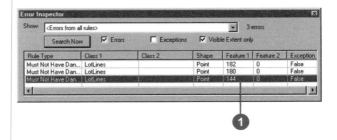

The feature flashes on the map, and the error feature turns black to show that it's selected.

2. Click and drag a small box around the error to zoom to the error.

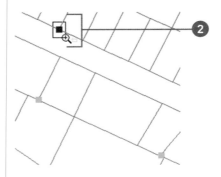

3. Zoom in again, if necessary, until you can see where the lot line with the error crosses the other lot line.

This is an overshoot error, a type of error that is often found in line work imported from CAD programs or digitized without using snapping to control the connectivity of the line features.

4. Right-click the error in the Error Inspector and click Trim.

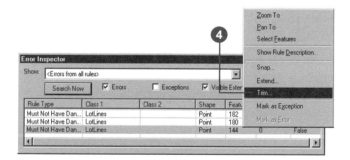

5. Type "3" in the Maximum Distance box and press Enter.

The dangling segment is trimmed back to where the lines intersect, and the error disappears.

The Error Inspector context menu provided a list of potential fixes for this error. You trimmed the line feature to fix this error. You also could have marked the error as an exception or snapped or extended the line until it reached another feature.

Correcting an undershoot error

Now you'll correct another type of dangle error.

1. Click the Go Back to Previous Extent button until you can see the two remaining errors in this area of the data.

2. Click the Zoom In tool and drag a box to zoom in to the westernmost of the two remaining errors.

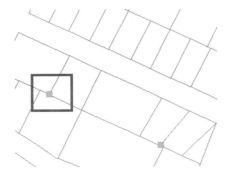

3. Zoom in again, if necessary, until you can see where the lot line with the error fails to connect to the other lot line.

This is an undershoot error, another type of error that is often found in line work imported from CAD programs

or digitized without using snapping to control the connectivity of the line features. The end of this line fell short by a little more than half a meter. You'll fix this error by extending the undershoot until it meets the line to which it should have been snapped.

4. Click the Fix Topology Error tool.

The Fix Topology Error tool lets you interactively select and apply predefined fixes to topology errors on the map.

5. Click and drag a box around the error.

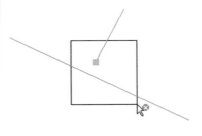

6. Right-click on the map and click Extend.

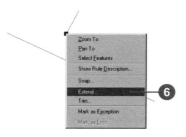

7. Type "3" in the Maximum Distance box and press Enter.

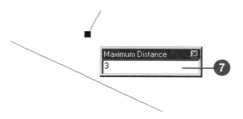

You've corrected the undershoot by extending the line with the dangle to the other line.

If the distance to the next line had been greater than the three-meter maximum distance you specified, the line would not have been extended.

Correcting a double-digitized line

Sometimes a given line or part of a line is digitized twice in the course of creating the data. This may happen with CAD drawings or with lines digitized on a digitizing tablet.

1. Click the Go Back to Previous Extent button until you can see the one remaining error in this area of the data.

2. Click the Zoom In tool and drag a box to zoom in to the remaining error.

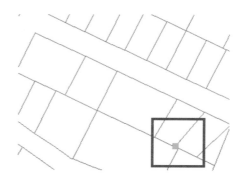

3. In the Error Inspector, click Search Now.

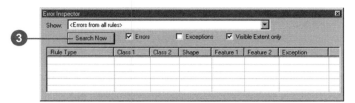

4. Click the numeric value in the Feature 1 column.

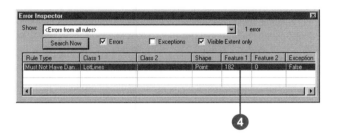

The line feature with the dangle flashes. Notice that the whole lot line did not flash.

5. Click and drag a box to zoom closer to the dangle error.

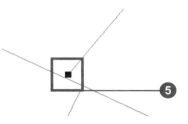

If necessary, zoom in again until you can see that there are two nearly parallel lot lines, one of which has the dangle.

You'll correct this error by deleting the extra line.

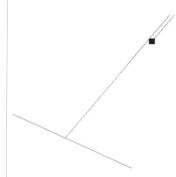

6. Right-click the numeric value in the Feature 1 column and click Select Features, then press the Delete key.

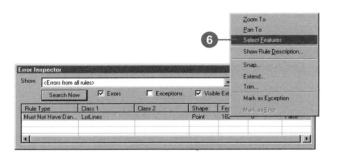

The extra line is deleted.

7. Click the Go Back to Previous Extent button until you can see the area in which you've been working.

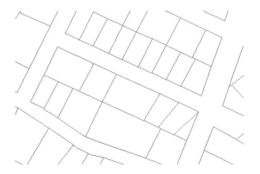

You've fixed three errors that resulted from violations of the Must Not Have Dangles rule. In each case the error was corrected by editing the geometry of a lot line feature by trimming, extending, or deleting the feature.

Topology errors are useful for tracking where there are problems with your data, but correcting the error requires you to correct the data—you can't edit the Topology error feature layer directly.

Reviewing the areas you've edited

When you edit features in a topology, the topology tracks where changes have been made. These places are called dirty areas because a topology rule could potentially have been violated by the edits, but the error, if it exists, cannot be found until the dirty area is validated again. When you validate the topology again, it just checks the dirty areas.

You can see the areas that have been edited by showing the dirty areas in the topology layer.

1. Click StudyArea_Topology in the ArcMap table of contents so only it is selected. Right-click it and click Properties.

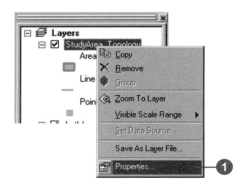

2. Click the Symbology tab.

3. Check Dirty Areas.

4. Click OK.

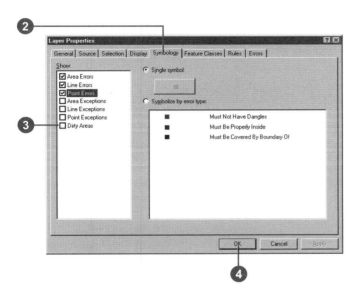

Now you can see the dirty areas on the map. The dirty areas cover the features that you edited. Dirty areas optimize the validation process, as only these must be checked for errors.

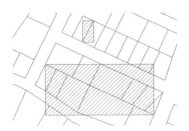

5. Click the Validate Topology in Specified Area tool.

6. Click and drag a box around the northern dirty area.

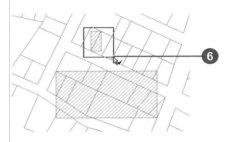

The dirty area is removed, and no errors are found in the area you validated.

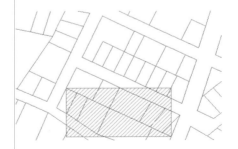

7. Click the Validate Topology in Current Extent button.

7

The topology is validated for the other areas you edited, and the dirty area is removed.

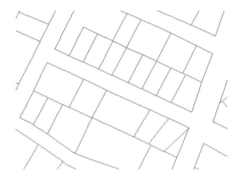

Creating a report of the status of the data

Next you'll generate a report summarizing the number of topology errors remaining in the data.

1. Right-click the topology in the ArcMap table of contents and click Properties.

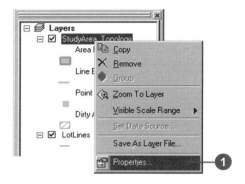

2. Click the Errors tab.

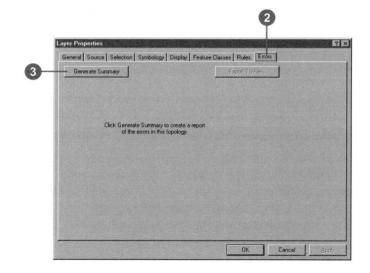

3. Click Generate Summary.

The summary shows the number of topology errors and exceptions; you may have a different number of errors. You could save this report to a text file to document the status of the data, but you do not need to do so for this exercise.

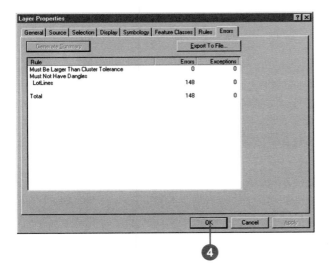

4. Click OK.

Fixing multiple errors at once

Many errors, like the double-digitized line, need to be fixed one at a time by deleting, modifying, or moving individual features. Some errors must be fixed by creating new features. However, sometimes a feature class contains a number of errors, such as the overshoots and undershoots, that are simple to fix. When this is the case, you can select multiple errors at once with the Fix Topology Error tool

and apply the same fix to all of them. If you prefer, you can individually check each error using the Error Inspector. This is a work flow and quality assurance decision that your organization should make before you begin applying topology fixes to multiple errors.

Before applying a fix to multiple errors, it's a good idea to look at your data and evaluate whether the fixes are appropriate. You would not want to trim lines with dangles that actually needed to be snapped to another line, or extend a line that actually needed to be trimmed.

In this case, if you extend dangling lines that are within three meters of another line, you're not likely to cause problems with your data, since the parcels and rights-of-way are larger than three meters.

Now you'll use this method to clean up several errors at one time.

1. Click the Full Extent button.

2. Click the Fix Topology Error tool.

3. Click and drag a box around all of the errors on the map.

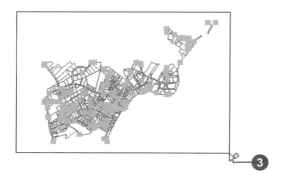

This selects all of the errors. Now you'll fix the undershoots.

4. Right-click on the map and click Extend.

5. The Maximum Distance you set when you fixed the other undershoot is fine, so press Enter.

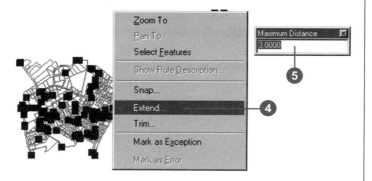

The process may take a few seconds while all of the features with dangles are checked to see if there is a feature within three meters to which they can be extended.

The undershoots are fixed, and a number of dirty areas appear on the map. Each dirty area marks the bounding box of a feature that was edited by the extend error fix.

6. Click Search Now on the Error Inspector.

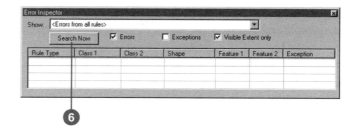

The number of topology errors is displayed to the right of the Show dropdown menu; you may have a different number of errors remaining. You will notice that many have been fixed. You could continue fixing topology errors to clean up this data, but you'll skip ahead in the process now, to see some other ways to clean up data with topology.

The number of errors
still remaining

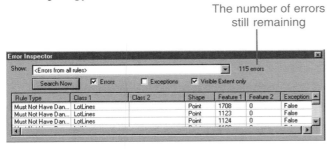

7. Click the Editor menu and click Stop Editing.

8. Click Yes to save your edits.

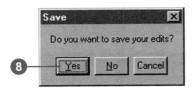

9. Close ArcMap.

Creating a new polygon feature class

Now you'll create a new feature class of Lot polygons from the lot lines feature class that you've been working on and from a point feature class that will supply the attributes of the new lot features.

1. Right-click the StudyArea dataset in ArcCatalog, point to New and click Polygon Feature Class From Lines.

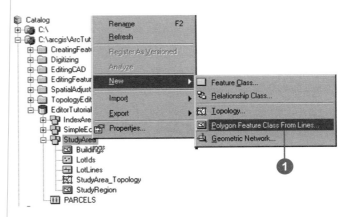

2. Type "Lots" as the new feature class's name.

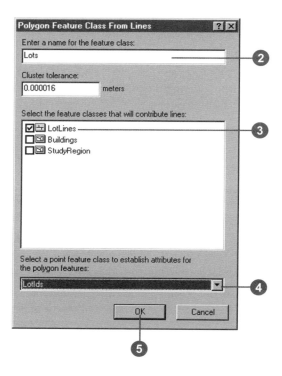

3. Check LotLines.
4. Click the point feature class dropdown list and click LotIds.
5. Click OK.

The new Lots polygon feature class is added to the StudyArea dataset. Next, you will include the Lots and LotIds feature classes in the topology so you can add rules to help you continue to clean up the data.

Adding feature classes to the topology

Before you can add topology rules for feature classes, you need to add the feature classes to the topology.

It is important to note that you are using this topology for the purpose of improving the polygon feature class you created from line work and points. You do not need to have the line or point feature classes to model the Lots—some organizations might decide to keep the LotLine feature class to provide easy annotation of lot boundary lengths, while others might not. Likewise, the Lots Parcel_ID attribute is now stored in the polygon feature class—you're using the LotIds feature class to quality check the data you've created. You might well decide not to keep the LotIds feature class when you've finished checking the data.

1. Right-click StudyArea_Topology and click Properties.

2. Click the Feature Classes tab.

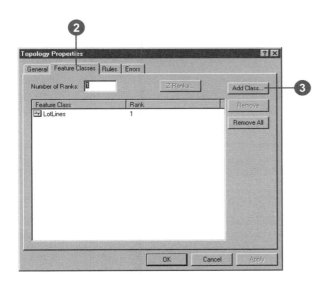

3. Click Add Class.

4. Click LotIds, press and hold the Ctrl key, and click Lots.

5. Click OK.

   Now that you've added these two feature classes to the topology, you can include them in topology rules.

Adding rules to the topology

1. Click the Rules tab.

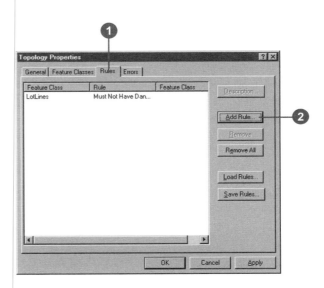

2. Click Add Rule.

3. Click the Features of feature class dropdown arrow and click LotIds.

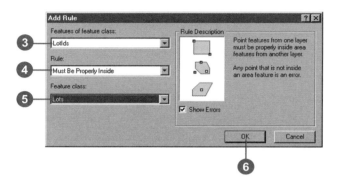

4. Click the Rule dropdown arrow and click Must be Properly Inside.

5. Click the Feature class dropdown arrow and click Lots.

6. Click OK.

This rule will be useful for finding places where lot polygons were not formed due to breaks in the line work.

7. Click Add Rule.

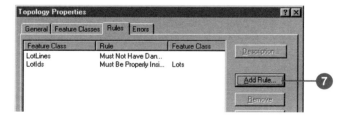

8. Click the Features of feature class dropdown arrow and click LotLines.

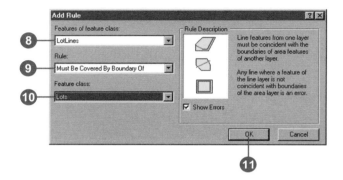

9. Click the Rule dropdown arrow and click Must be Covered By Boundary Of.

10. Click the Feature class dropdown arrow and click Lots.

11. Click OK.

This rule will be useful for finding polygons that were not completely split due to gaps in the line work.

12. Click OK.

13. Right-click StudyArea_Topology and click Validate.

You've added two more feature classes to the topology and added topology rules to control their spatial relationships.

Adding the new topology to ArcMap

Now you'll examine the revised topology in ArcMap and continue cleaning up your data.

1. Start ArcMap.

2. Click and drag the topology from ArcCatalog onto ArcMap.

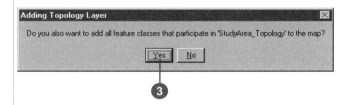

3. Click Yes to add all of the feature classes that participate in the topology to the map.

The topology and the feature classes that participate in it are added to the map.

4. Click the Zoom In tool.

5. Click and drag a box around the central part of the south edge of the data.

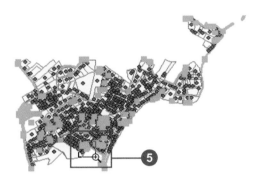

Now there are line and point errors visible on the map.

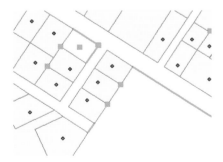

The red lines represent a new type of error feature—line errors. These show violations of the Must Be Covered

By Boundary Of rule. There are two types of point errors now, violations of the Must Not Have Dangles rule, which you're already familiar with, and violations of the Must Be Properly Inside rule.

Changing a point error symbol

Since there is now more than one type of point error, you will change the symbology of the Topology layer to make it clearer which errors are which.

1. Click StudyArea_Topology in the ArcMap table of contents so only it is selected. Right-click it and click Properties.

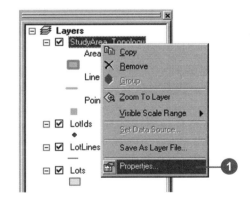

2. Click the Symbology tab.

3. Click Point Errors.

4. Double-click the square symbol for Must Be Properly Inside errors.

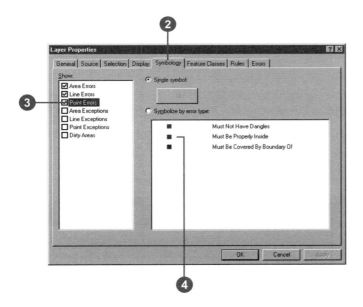

5. Click a triangle symbol and set the color to red.

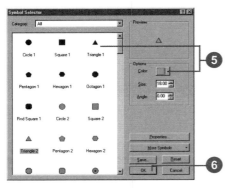

6. Click OK.

7. Double-click each of the square symbols for the other two errors and set their colors to Medium Coral Light.

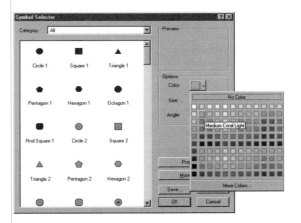

8. Click OK on all dialog boxes.

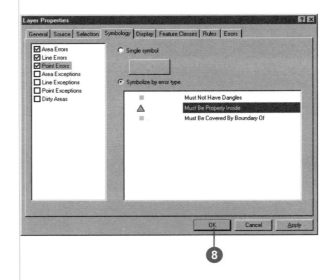

The triangle marks the LotID point for a lot that was not created when you created polygons from lines. The red square to the east of the triangle is actually a pair of dangles where the lot lines were not snapped together. The two lot lines are marked as errors because they are not covered by a lot polygon boundary.

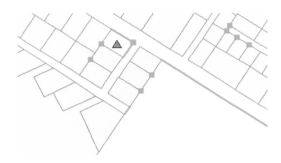

1. Click Editor and click Start Editing.

2. Click the Error Inspector button.

3. Click Search Now.

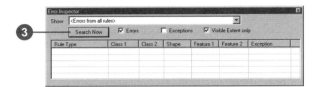

The visible extent of your map will determine how many errors you see.

4. Click the Show dropdown list and click LotIds - Must Be Properly Inside - Lots.

5. Click Search Now.

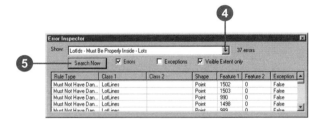

Now you can see the one violation of this rule visible in this part of the data. You can use the Error Inspector to sort through the various types of topology errors in your map.

6. Uncheck Visible Extent only.

7. Click Search Now.

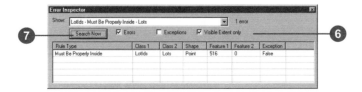

There are several violations of this rule in the topology. After you fix this error, you could use the Error Inspector to systematically find the other LotIDs that are not within Lot polygons, although for this exercise you will not.

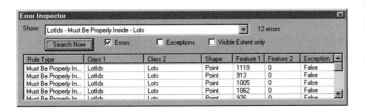

8. Right-click a feature in the Error Inspector table and click Pan To.

   The map pans to the error you selected.

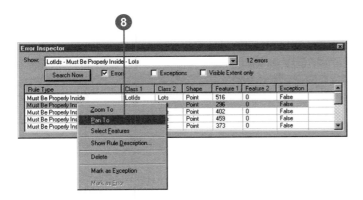

Now you'll go back to the error you were just looking at and fix it.

9. Click the Go Back to Previous Extent button.

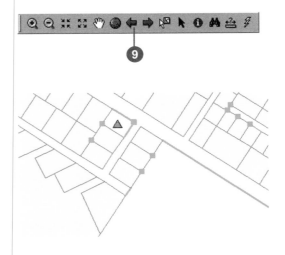

Creating a new polygon

Now you will create the new lot and fix these topology errors.

1. Click the Target dropdown arrow on the Editor toolbar and click Lots.

2. Press Alt+R and press N.

   The key combination Alt+R opens the Editor menu, and N opens the Snapping Environment dialog box.

3. Check the End box for LotLines and close the dialog box.

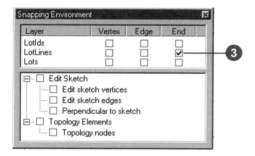

4. Click the Edit tool.

5. Hold the Z key and drag a box around the place where the lot lines should intersect.

6. Double-click the northern lot line, move the pointer over its eastern end until the pointer changes to a box with four arrows, click the end, and drag it east until it snaps to the other lot line.

7. Click the Go Back to Previous Extent button.

You should be able to see the lot lines and the lot polygons that adjoin this lot to the south and west. Now the new polygon can be constructed.

8. Hold the Shift key and click the eastern lot line.

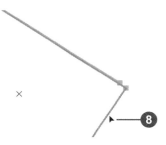

Both northern and eastern lot lines should now be selected.

9. Click the Construct Features tool.

10. Check the box to consider existing features.

11. Click OK.

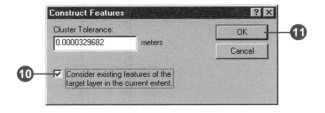

The new Lot polygon feature is created from the selected lines and from the existing Lot polygon boundaries.

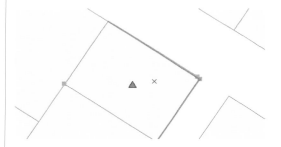

12. Click the Validate Topology in Current Extent button.

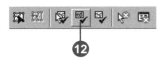

The new polygon covers the LotID point, the polygon boundary covers the lot lines, and you fixed the dangle errors by snapping them together, so when you validated the topology in the area, all of those errors went away.

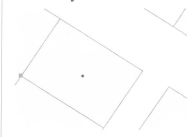

It is important to note that the new polygon has a <null> value for its Parcel_ID attribute. The other parcels, which you created in ArcCatalog, derived their Parcel_ID attribute values from the LotID point feature class. There are several ways that you could add this information to the new parcel. You could edit the parcel's attributes and type in its Lot_ID value. You could select the LotID point feature and the Lot polygon, open the Attributes dialog box, and copy and paste the Parcel_ID value from one to the other. You could even use the Attribute Transfer tool on the Spatial Adjustment toolbar to transfer the attributes from the point to the polygon.

For this exercise you'll skip updating the new polygon feature's attributes and move on to edit another Lot polygon.

Splitting a polygon

Because there were some undershoot dangle errors with gaps larger than three meters, there are some lots that were not completely enclosed. Where the gap opened onto an adjacent lot, and the two lots' other boundaries were closed, a single large lot was created. In this step you'll split up one such lot.

1. Click the Full Extent button.

2. Hold the Z key and drag a box around the lots on the south side of the eastern part of the study area.

3. Click one of the lots that are on either side of the Must Be Covered By Boundary Of line error.

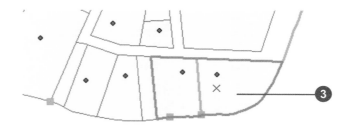

The lots are incorrectly represented by a single feature. The error at the south end of the line error is an undershoot dangle error. You'll use a new method to fix this error using a tool on the Advanced Editing toolbar.

4. Click Editor, point to More Editing Tools, and click Advanced Editing.

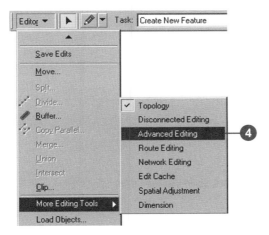

The Advanced Editing toolbar appears.

5. Click the Extend tool.

The Extend tool works differently from the Extend topology error fix. Rather than specifying a distance, you select a feature to which the tool will extend a line. After a feature is selected, you click the line feature that you want to extend. Since the parcel is currently selected, all you have to do is click the dangling lot line. You'll zoom in a little closer to see the gap.

6. Press and hold the Z key and drag a box around the line near the south edge of the parcel.

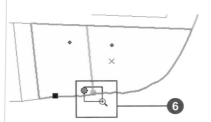

7. Move the pointer over the dangling end of the line.

When the pointer gets close to the endpoint, the blue circle snaps to it. Although you can click anywhere on the line that you want to extend, the Extend tool obeys the current snapping environment. Since you set up snapping to endpoints of LotLines earlier, the Extend tool snaps to them.

8. Click the line.

The line is extended to the nearest selected feature—in this case, the edge of the Lot polygon.

9. Click the Go Back to Previous Extent button.

10. Click the Select Features tool.

11. Click and drag a box around the line that you just extended.

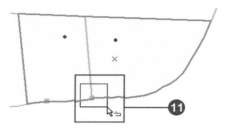

This also selects the parcel.

12. Click the Construct Features tool.

13. Check the box to Consider existing features.

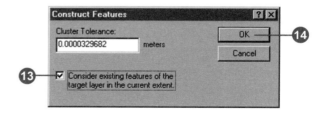

14. Click OK.

The newly extended line feature splits the existing parcel into two features.

15. Click the Validate Topology in Current Extent button.

The topology is validated and the line error and dangle are removed.

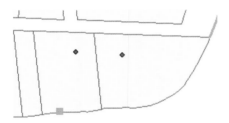

You will need to check the attributes of both of these lots against the attributes of the LotIds points and update one or both of them to make sure that they have the right PARCEL_ID numbers. The new lot feature has a <null> PARCEL_ID, and there is a 50 percent chance that the wrong parcel inherited the value from the original large parcel.

There are many more errors in the data, although as you saw in this and the previous examples, more than one error may be related to a given problem. Almost all of the errors follow from the underlying problem of the original CAD data, incompletely snapped line work, and unclosed polygons. Spending more time editing the dangle errors would have taken care of most of the errors that were revealed by adding the new rules.

Some of the errors, like the small dangling line and the lot line not covered by a parcel boundary visible here, may not need to be corrected at all. If your organization needs only to model lots, the LotLine and LotIDs feature classes could be removed from the topology and deleted once you've finished developing the polygon features from them. On the other hand, you might want to keep the lot lines for cartographic reasons or to simplify annotating the dimensions of lots. If this is the case, you would need to continue cleaning up the lot lines. An additional step would be to use the Planarize Lines tool to split all of the lot lines at intersections—something that was not done with the original CAD data. The two errors visible above are actually on the same feature. Planarizing the lines would split this feature into several features, each tracing a single lot boundary.

Whether or not you retain the LotLines and LotIds feature classes, you would probably want to add at least one more rule to assist in the day-to-day management of the lot feature class. One such rule would be a Must Not Overlap rule, so when you digitize new lots they cannot overlap each other. This should not be a problem for the lots you've just created, but it is a rule that one would typically enforce on landownership polygons.

In this exercise you have created a geodatabase topology with simple rules to help you clean up data. You have learned how to use the Error Inspector to find errors of a particular type and how to use some of the many editing tools to fix errors in your data.

Exercise 8: Using the Spatial Adjustment tool

The Spatial Adjustment tool allows you to transform, rubbersheet, and edgematch your data within an edit session.

Spatial adjustments are based on displacement links. These are special graphical elements that represent the source and destination locations for an adjustment.

This exercise will show you how to perform each of the spatial adjustments.

Starting ArcMap and beginning editing

Before you can complete the tasks in this tutorial, you must start ArcMap and load the tutorial data.

1. Double-click a shortcut installed on your desktop or use the Programs list in your Start menu to start ArcMap.

2. Click the Open button on the Standard toolbar. Navigate to the Transform.mxd map document in the Editor directory where you installed the tutorial data. (C:\ArcGIS\ArcTutor is the default location.)

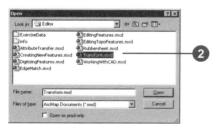

3. If the Editor toolbar isn't displayed in ArcMap, click the Editor Toolbar button on the Standard toolbar to add it.

4. Click Editor and click Start Editing.

Adding the Spatial Adjustment toolbar

1. Click the View menu, point to Toolbars, and click Spatial Adjustment to add the Spatial Adjustment toolbar to ArcMap.

The Spatial Adjustment toolbar appears.

Setting the snapping environment

Before you start adding links, you should set your snapping environment so each link you add snaps to the vertices or endpoints of features. For more information about snapping, see the 'Creating new features' chapter in *Editing in ArcMap*.

1. Click the Editor menu and click Snapping to display the Snapping Environment dialog box.

2. Check the Vertex check box next to the NewParcels and SimpleParcels layers to snap the displacement links to the vertices of these features. Close the dialog box.

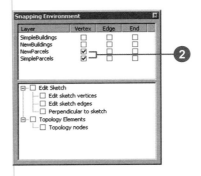

Applying a transformation

A transformation is used to convert the coordinates of a layer from one location to another. This involves the scaling, shifting, and rotation of features based on displacement links defined by the user. Transformations are applied uniformly to all features in a feature class and are often used to convert data created in digitizer units into real-world units represented on a map. For more information on transformations, see the 'Spatial adjustment' chapter in *Editing in ArcMap*.

This exercise will show you how to apply a transformation based on displacement links that you will create. This transformation will move, scale, and rotate two feature classes containing parcel and building features into alignment with another set of parcel and building feature classes. You might use this technique to adjust data that was digitized or imported into a temporary feature class in preparation for copying and pasting the features into your database. You will also learn how to specify which features to adjust, preview the adjustment, and view a link table.

Specifying the features to adjust

The Spatial Adjustment tool allows you to adjust a selected set of features or all the features in a layer. This setting is available in the Choose Input For Adjustment dialog box. For geodatabase feature classes and shapefiles, the default is to adjust a selected set of features.

1. Click the Spatial Adjustment menu and click Set Adjust Data to display the Choose Input For Adjustment window.

2. Check the All features in these layers check box.

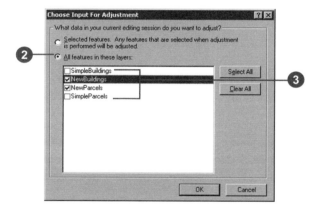

3. Uncheck the SimpleBuildings and SimpleParcels layers, keep the NewBuildings and NewParcels layers checked, and click OK.

Selecting an adjustment method

Now that you have determined which features will be adjusted, the next step is to choose an adjustment method. The Spatial Adjustment tool supports several adjustment methods. In this exercise, you will perform a Similarity Transformation. For more information on adjustment methods, see the 'Spatial adjustment' chapter in *Editing in ArcMap*.

1. Click the Spatial Adjustment menu, point to Adjustment Methods, and click Transformation - Similarity to set the adjustment method.

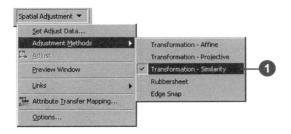

Adding displacement links

Displacement links define the source and destination coordinates for an adjustment. Displacement links can be created manually or loaded from a link file. In this exercise, you will create your own displacement links from the exterior corners of the NewParcels layer to the corresponding locations in the SimpleParcels layer.

1. Click the New Displacement Link tool on the Spatial Adjustment toolbar.

2. With the New Displacement tool active, snap to a from-point in the source layer and snap to a to-point in the target layer.

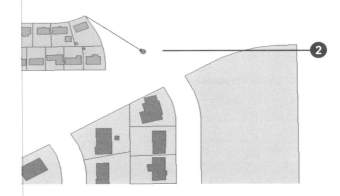

3. Continue to create additional links as shown below. For this exercise, you should have a total of four displacement links when you are finished.

Examining the adjustment

The Spatial Adjustment tool includes a tool to preview an adjustment prior to actually performing the adjustment. This tool is called the Preview Window. If the results of the adjustment are not adequate, you can modify the links to improve the accuracy of the adjustment.

1. Click the Spatial Adjustment menu and click Preview Window.

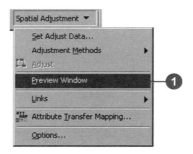

The Adjustment Preview Window appears.

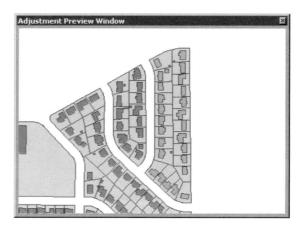

In addition to the visual preview of the adjustment, you can also examine the results of the adjustment by viewing the Link Table. The Link Table provides information about link coordinates, link IDs, and RMS errors.

2. Click the View Link Table button on the Spatial Adjustment toolbar.

The Link Table dialog box appears.

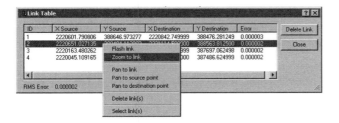

Right-clicking a link record opens the Link Table's context menu. You can edit link coordinates, flash links, zoom and pan to selected links, and delete links with these commands.

For more information on RMS errors, see the 'Spatial adjustment' chapter in *Editing in ArcMap*.

If the RMS error for this adjustment is not acceptable, you can modify the links to increase the accuracy. The Preview Window and Link Table tools are designed to help you fine-tune your adjustment.

Performing the adjustment

The final step of the spatial adjustment process is to perform the adjustment.

1. Click the Spatial Adjustment menu and click Adjust.

Since the Spatial Adjustment tool operates in an edit session, you can use the Undo command to undo the adjustment.

The adjusted data should look like this:

Saving your edits

If you are satisfied with the results of the spatial adjustment, you can stop editing and save your edits.

1. Click Editor and click Stop Editing.

2. Click Yes to save your edits.

In this exercise, you learned how to set your data for an adjustment, create displacement links, preview the adjustment, and use the Link table to view the RMS error. For more information about the Spatial Adjustment tool, see the 'Spatial adjustment' chapter in *Editing in ArcMap*.

Rubbersheeting your data

Rubbersheeting is typically used to align two or more layers. This process moves the features of a layer using a piecewise transformation that preserves straight lines.

This exercise will show you how to rubbersheet data by using displacement links, multiple displacement links, and identity links. You will rubbersheet a newly imported set of street features to match an existing feature class of street features.

This tutorial assumes that ArcMap is started and the Editor and Spatial Adjustment toolbars have been added to ArcMap.

1. Close the Transformation.mxd map document.

2. Click the Open button on the Standard toolbar. Navigate to the Rubbersheet.mxd map document in the Editor directory where you installed the tutorial data. (C:\ArcGIS\ArcTutor is the default location.)

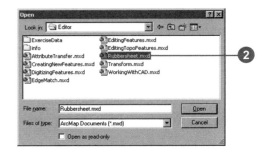

3. Click Editor and click Start Editing.

Setting the snapping environment

Before you start creating links, you should set your snapping environment so each link you add snaps to the vertices or endpoints of features. For more information about snapping, see *Editing in ArcMap*.

1. Click the Editor menu and click Snapping to display the Snapping Environment dialog box.

2. Check the Vertex check box next to the ImportStreets and Streets layers to snap the displacement links to the vertices of these features. Close the dialog box.

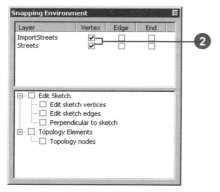

Setting data for the adjustment

The Spatial Adjustment tool allows you to adjust a selected set of features or all the features in a layer. This setting is available in the Choose Input For Adjustment dialog box. The default is to adjust selected features.

1. Click the Spatial Adjustment menu and click Set Adjust Data to display the Choose Input For Adjustment dialog box.

2. Check the All features in these layers check box.

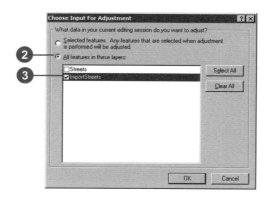

3. Uncheck the Streets layer. Keep the ImportStreets layer checked, then click OK.

Selecting an adjustment method

Now that you have determined which features will be adjusted, the next step is to choose an adjustment method. The Spatial Adjustment tool supports several adjustment methods. In this exercise, you will use Rubbersheet.

1. Click the Spatial Adjustment menu, point to Adjustment Methods, then click Rubbersheet to set the adjustment method.

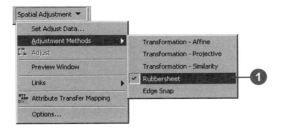

2. Next, click the Spatial Adjustment menu and click Options to open the Adjustment Properties dialog box.

3. Click the General tab, then click Rubbersheet from the Adjustment method dropdown list.

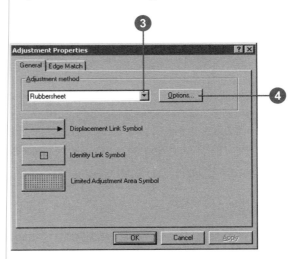

4. Click Options to choose a rubbersheet method.

5. Click the Natural Neighbor method and click OK.

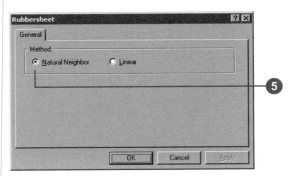

6. Click OK to close the Adjustment Properties dialog box.

Locating the adjust data

Spatial bookmarks are named extents that can be saved in map documents. Creating a bookmark for areas that you visit frequently will save you time. For information on how to create and manage spatial bookmarks, see *Using ArcMap*.

You will now zoom to a spatial bookmark created for this exercise.

1. Click the View menu, point to Bookmarks, then click Import streets to set the current view to the edit area of this exercise.

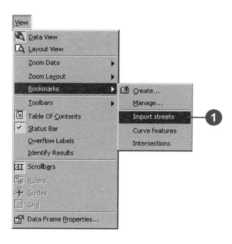

When the display refreshes, note that the ImportStreets layer is not aligned with the Streets layer. You must adjust the ImportStreets layer so it aligns with the Streets layer by using the rubbersheet adjustment method.

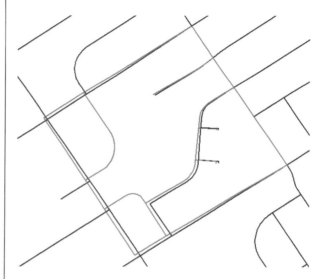

2. To get a better view of the adjustment area, you need to zoom to the bookmark called Intersections, which was created for you. Click the View menu, point to Bookmarks, then click Intersections.

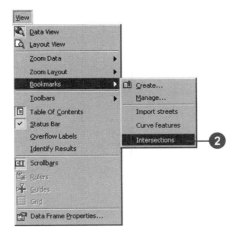

Adding displacement links

Displacement links define the source and destination coordinates for an adjustment. Displacement links can be created manually or loaded from a link file. In this exercise, you will create your own displacement links at several key intersections of the Streets and ImportStreets layers.

1. Click the New Displacement Link tool on the Spatial Adjustment toolbar.

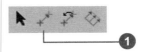

2. Snap the link to the source location in the ImportStreets layer, as shown below.

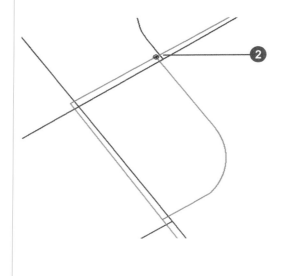

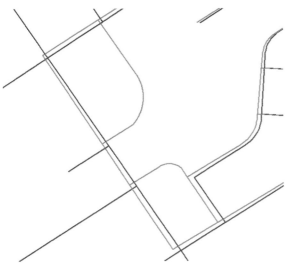

3. Snap the link to the destination location in the Streets layer, as shown below.

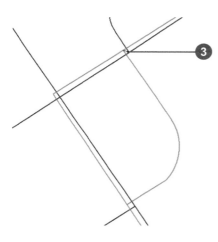

4. Continue to create links at the perimeter intersections of the layers in a counterclockwise direction. You will create a total of six displacement links, as shown below.

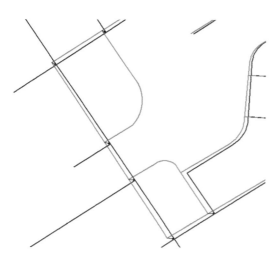

Adding multidisplacement links

The Multiple Displacement Links tool allows you to create multiple displacement links in one operation. This tool can help save time by allowing you to create more than one link at a time; it is especially useful for curved features.

1. To get a better view of the adjustment area, zoom to the bookmark called Curve features, which was created for you. Click the View menu, point to Bookmarks, and click Curve features.

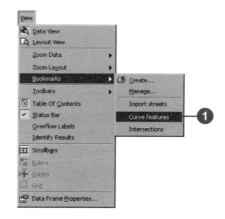

To preserve the curved road features, add multiple links at critical points.

2. Click the Multiple Displacement Links tool on the Spatial Adjustment toolbar.

3. With the Multiple Displacement Links tool active, click the curved road feature in the ImportStreets layer.

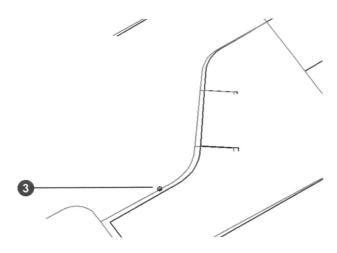

4. With the Multiple Displacement Links tool still active, click the curved road feature in the Streets layer.

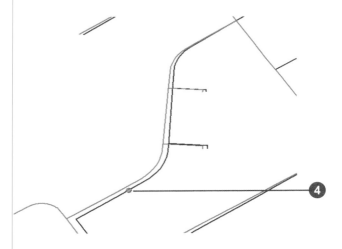

5. You will be prompted to enter the number of links to create. Accept the default value (10) and press Enter.

The multiple links now appear in the map.

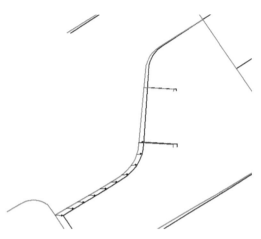

6. Use the Multiple Displacement Links tool to create multiple links for the remaining curved feature.

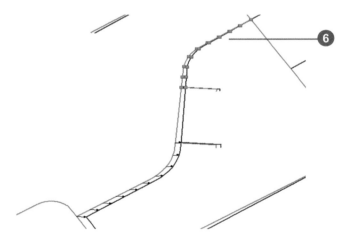

7. Click the New Displacement Link tool on the Spatial Adjustment toolbar.

8. Add the final displacement links, as shown below:

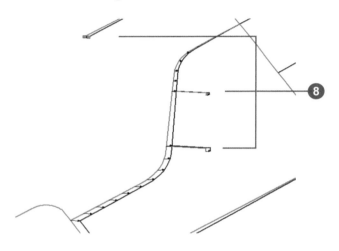

Adding identity links

Identity links are used to anchor features at specific points to prevent their movement during an adjustment. You will now add identity links at key intersections to maintain their locations.

1. Click the New Identity Link tool on the Spatial Adjustment toolbar.

2. With the New Identity Link tool active, add five identity links at the intersections shown below.

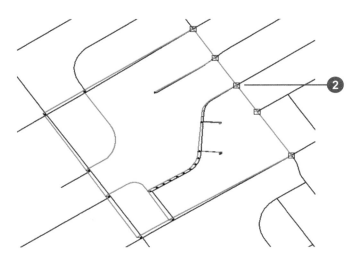

Examining the adjustment

You can examine how an adjustment will appear prior to actually performing it with the Preview Window. Use the standard ArcMap Zoom and Pan tools to change the display of the Preview Window.

1. Click the Spatial Adjustment menu and click Preview Window to examine the adjustment.

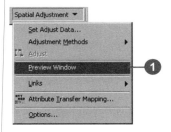

The Adjustment Preview Window appears.

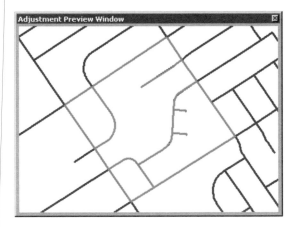

If the results are not acceptable, modify the existing links to improve the accuracy of the adjustment.

Performing the adjustment

The final step of the spatial adjustment process is to perform the adjustment.

1. Click the Spatial Adjustment menu and click Adjust.

Since the Spatial Adjustment tool operates in an edit session, you can use the Undo command to undo the adjustment. Here is how the adjustment should appear:

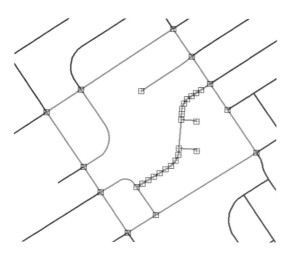

After performing the rubbersheet adjustment, you will notice that all of the displacement links you created have turned into Identity links. The next step is to delete these links since you no longer need them.

1. Click the Select Elements tool on the Spatial Adjustment toolbar. This will allow you to select the links since they are graphic elements.

2. Click the Edit menu and click Select All Elements.

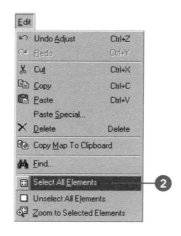

3. Press the Delete key.

Saving your edits

If you are satisfied with the results of the spatial adjustment, you can stop editing and save your edits.

1. Click the Editor menu and click Stop Editing.

2. Click Yes to save your edits.

In this exercise, you learned how to set your data for an adjustment, create displacement links, create identity links, and preview the adjustment. For more information about the Spatial Adjustment tool, see the 'Spatial adjustment' chapter in *Editing in ArcMap*.

Edgematching data

Edgematching is used to align features along the edges of adjacent layers. Usually, the layer with the less accurate features is adjusted, while the other layer is used as the target layer. Edgematching relies on displacement links to define the adjustment.

In this exercise you will edgematch two adjacent tiles of stream data by using displacement links that you will create. You will also learn how to use the Edge Match tool and set Edge Snap properties.

This tutorial assumes that ArcMap is started and the Editor and Spatial Adjustment toolbars have been added to ArcMap.

1. Close the Rubbersheet.mxd map document.

2. Click the Open button on the Standard toolbar. Navigate to the EdgeMatch.mxd map document in the Editor directory where you installed the tutorial data. (C:\ArcGIS\ArcTutor is the default location.)

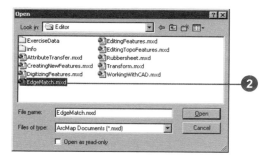

3. Click Editor and click Start Editing.

Setting the snapping environment

Before you start creating links, you should set your snapping environment so each link you add snaps to the vertices or endpoints of features. For more information about snapping, see *Editing in ArcMap*.

1. Click the Editor menu and click Snapping to display the Snapping Environment window.

2. Check the End check boxes next to the StreamsNorth and StreamsSouth layers to snap the displacement links to the endpoints of these features. Close the dialog box.

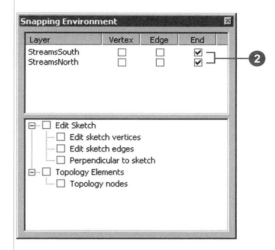

Setting data for the adjustment

The Spatial Adjustment tool allows you to adjust a selected set of features or all the features in a layer. This setting is available in the Choose Input For Adjustment dialog box. The default is to adjust a selected set of features.

1. Click the Spatial Adjustment menu and click Set Adjust Data to display the Choose Input For Adjustment dialog box.

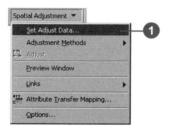

2. Click Selected features and click OK.

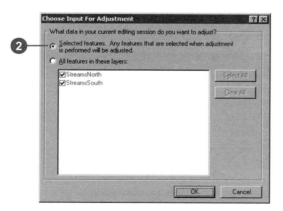

Choosing an adjustment method

Now that you have determined which features will be adjusted, the next step is to choose an adjustment method. The Spatial Adjustment tool supports several adjustment methods. In this exercise, you will use Edge Snap.

1. Click the Spatial Adjustment menu, point to Adjustment Methods, then click Edge Snap to set the adjustment method.

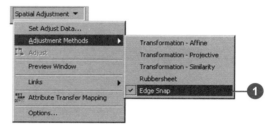

2. Click the Spatial Adjustment menu and click Options to open the Adjustment Properties dialog box.

   You will define several edgematch settings and properties in this dialog box.

Setting the adjustment method properties

1. Click the General tab, then click the Adjustment method dropdown arrow and click Edge Snap as your adjustment method.

2. Click Options to open the Edge Snap dialog box.

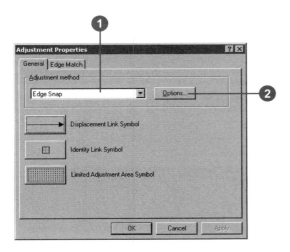

3. Click Line as the method and click OK.

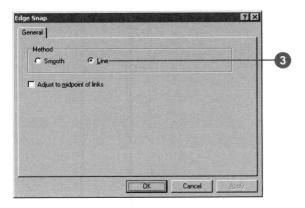

The line method only moves the endpoint of the line being adjusted. The Smooth method distributes the adjustment across the entire feature.

Setting the edgematch properties

The edgematch adjustment method requires additional adjustment methods. These properties will define the source and target layers as well as determine how the displacement links will be created when using the Edge Match tool.

1. Click the Edge Match tab of the Adjustment Properties dialog box.

2. Click the Source Layer dropdown arrow and click StreamsNorth.

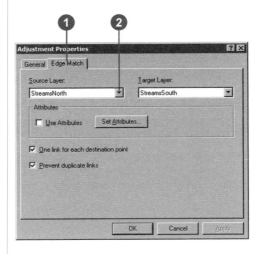

3. Click the Target Layer dropdown arrow and click StreamsSouth.

The StreamsNorth layer will be adjusted to match the target layer, StreamsSouth.

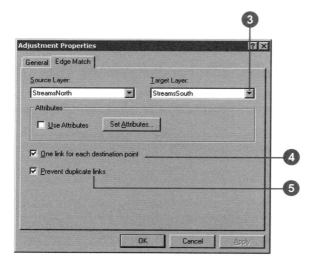

4. Check the One link for each destination point check box.

5. Click the Prevent duplicate links check box and click OK.

Locating the adjust data

You will now zoom to a spatial bookmark created for this exercise.

1. Click the View menu, point to Bookmarks, then click West streams to set the current view to the edit area of this exercise.

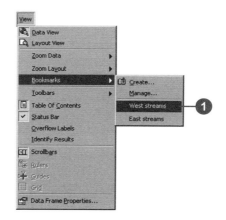

The map will display the following area:

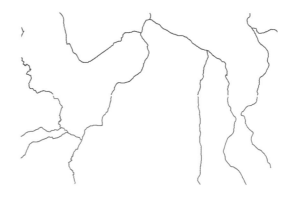

Adding displacement links

Displacement links define the source and destination coordinates for an adjustment. In this exercise, you will create multiple links using the Edge Match tool.

1. Click the Edge Match tool on the Spatial Adjustment toolbar.

2. With the Edge Match tool active, drag a box around the endpoints of the features.

   The Edge Match tool will create multiple displacement links based on the source and target features that fall inside the box.

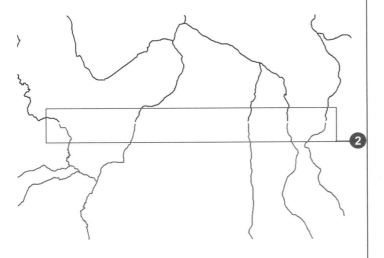

Displacement links now connect the source and target features at their endpoints.

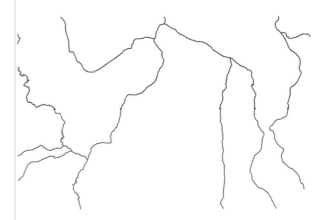

Selecting features

Since edgematching only affects the exterior regions of the layer, you must select the features that you want to adjust.

1. Click the Edit tool on the Editor toolbar.

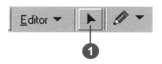

2. With the Edit tool active, drag a box around the features that are to be edgematched, as shown below.

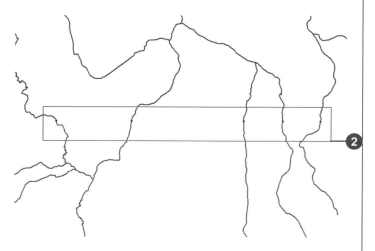

The participating features are now selected.

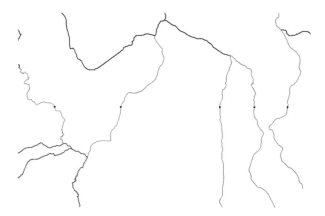

Adding additional displacement links

1. Click the View menu, point to Bookmarks, then click East streams.

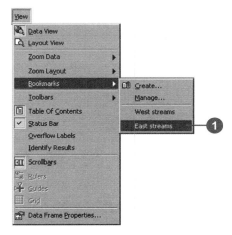

Repeat the same steps used for creating links with the Edge Match tool for the East streams portion of the data.

You will need to hold the Shift key while you select the stream features so the features from the West side stay selected.

Examining the adjustment

You can examine how an adjustment will appear prior to actually performing it with the Preview Window. You can use the standard ArcMap Zoom and Pan tools to change the display of the Preview Window.

1. Click the Spatial Adjustment menu and click Preview Window to examine the adjustment.

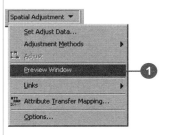

The following window appears:

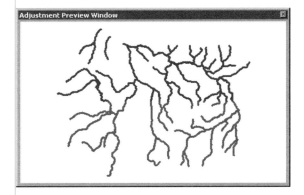

If the results are not acceptable, you can modify the existing links to improve the accuracy of the adjustment.

Performing the adjustment

The final step of the spatial adjustment process is to perform the adjustment.

1. Click the Spatial Adjustment menu and click Adjust.

Since the Spatial Adjustment tool operates in an edit session, you can use the Undo command to undo the adjustment. Here is how the adjustment should appear:

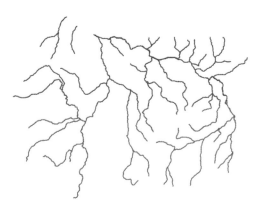

Saving your edits

If you are satisfied with the results of the spatial adjustment, you can stop editing and save your edits.

1. Click the Editor menu and click Stop Editing.

2. Click Yes to save your edits.

In this exercise, you learned how to set edgematch properties, use the Edge Match tool to create displacement links, and preview the adjustment. For more information about the Spatial Adjustment tool, see the 'Spatial adjustment' chapter in *Editing in ArcMap*.

Exercise 9: Using the Attribute Transfer tool

The Attribute Transfer tool is used to transfer attributes from features in a source layer to features in a target layer. Source and target layers and the attributes to be transferred are defined in the Attribute Transfer Mapping dialog box. The Attribute Transfer tool is then used to interactively transfer those attributes between features of the source and target layers.

In this exercise you'll transfer the street name and type from an existing street to a new street recently added to the database.

Starting ArcMap and beginning editing

Before you can complete the tasks in this tutorial, you must start ArcMap and load the tutorial data.

1. Double-click a shortcut installed on your desktop or use the Programs list in your Start menu to start ArcMap.

2. Click the Open button on the Standard toolbar. Navigate to the AttributeTransfer.mxd map document in the Editor directory where you installed the tutorial data. (C:\ArcGIS\ArcTutor is the default location.)

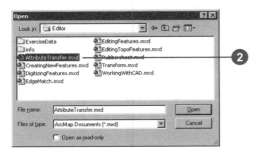

3. Click the Editor Toolbar button on the Standard toolbar to add the Editor toolbar to ArcMap.

4. Click the Editor menu and click Start Editing.

Adding the Spatial Adjustment toolbar

1. Click the View menu, point to Toolbars, then click Spatial Adjustment to add the Spatial Adjustment toolbar to ArcMap.

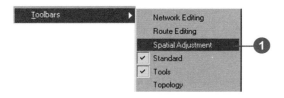

The Spatial Adjustment toolbar appears.

Setting the snapping environment

Before you transfer attributes, you should set your snapping environment for your source and target layers. This will ensure that you select the correct feature when using the Attribute Transfer tool. For more information about snapping, see *Editing in ArcMap*.

1. Click the Editor menu and click Snapping to display the Snapping Environment window.

2. Check the Edge check boxes next to the Streets and NewStreets layers. Close the dialog box.

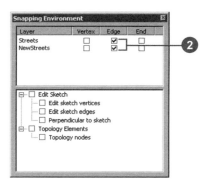

Setting the source and target layers

The first step in the Attribute Transfer process is to set the source and target layers. The Attribute Transfer Mapping dialog box allows you to define these settings.

1. Click the Spatial Adjustment menu and click Attribute Transfer Mapping.

2. Click the Source Layer dropdown arrow and click the Streets layer.

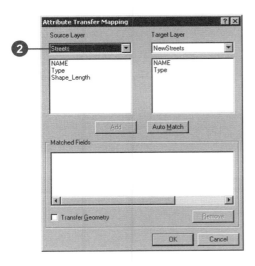

3. Click the Target Layer dropdown arrow and click the NewStreets layer.

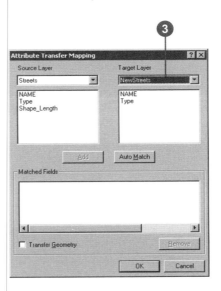

Mapping source and target fields

The next step is to specify which fields to use for the attribute transfer. You will select a field in the source layer and match it to a corresponding field in the target layer. The Attribute Transfer tool will use these matched fields to determine which data to transfer.

1. Click the NAME field in the Source Layer field list box.

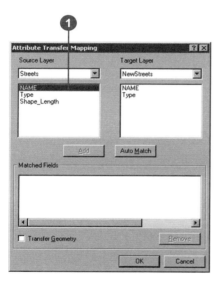

2. Click the NAME field in the Target Layer field list box.

3. Click Add.

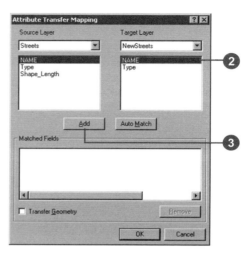

The fields are now added to the Matched Fields list box.

4. Repeat the same steps for the Type fields and click OK.

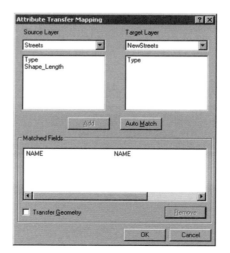

Locating the adjust data

Spatial bookmarks are named extents that can be saved in map documents. Creating a bookmark for areas that you visit frequently will save you time. For information on how to create and manage spatial bookmarks, see *Using ArcMap*.

You will now zoom to a spatial bookmark created for this exercise.

1. Click the View menu, point to Bookmarks, then click New streets to set the current view to the edit area of this exercise.

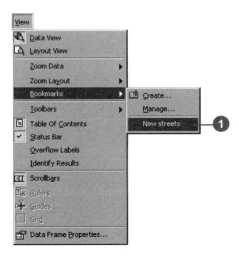

When the display refreshes, you should see the following area in your map:

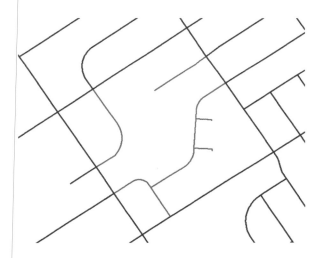

Identifying features for the attribute transfer

Prior to performing the attribute transfer, you will need to verify the attributes of the source and target features. This can be done using the Identify tool.

1. Click the Identify tool. The Identify Results dialog box appears.

2. Click the source feature indicated, as shown below.

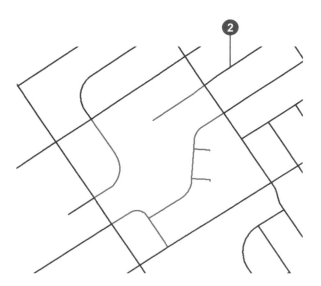

Notice the NAME and Type field attributes. These attribute values will be transferred to the target feature.

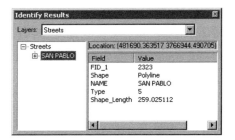

3. With the Identify tool still active, click the target feature, as shown below.

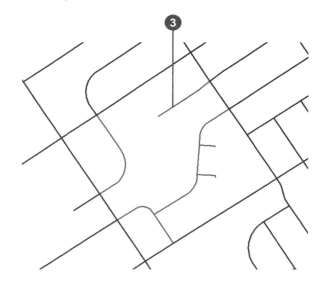

The Identify Results dialog box now displays
information about the target feature. Notice the NAME
and Type fields; attribute values for these fields will be
transferred to the target layer from the Streets layer.

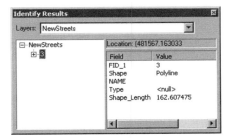

Using the Attribute Transfer tool

You will now use the Attribute Transfer tool to transfer the
source feature attributes to the target feature.

1. Click the Attribute Transfer tool on the Spatial
   Adjustment toolbar.

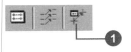

2. Snap to an edge of the source feature, as shown below.

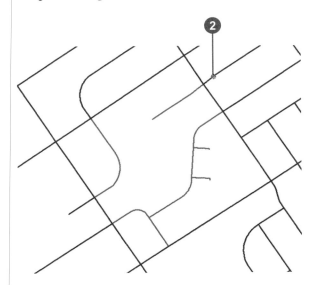

3. Drag the link toward the target feature.

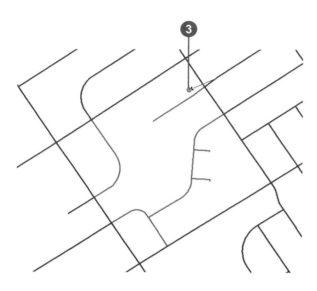

4. Snap to an edge of the target feature and click.

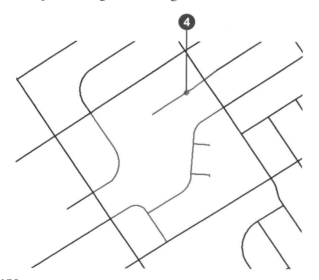

Verifying the results of the attribute transfer

Now that you have transferred the attributes from the source feature to the target feature, it is a good idea to verify that the target feature was updated with the proper information.

1. Click the Identify tool.

2. Click the target feature.

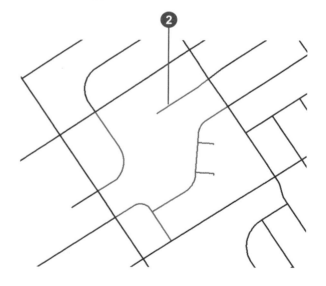

The NAME and Type fields in the target feature should reflect the new attributes:

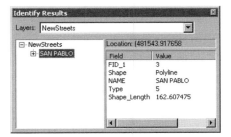

Transferring attributes to multiple features

To transfer the attributes of a source feature to multiple target features, hold down the Shift key while selecting the target features.

Saving your edits

If you are satisfied with the results of the attribute transfer, you can stop editing and save your edits.

1. Click the Editor menu and click Stop Editing.

2. Click Yes to save your edits.

In this exercise, you learned how to transfer attributes from a source layer to a target layer. For more information about the Attribute Transfer tool, see the 'Spatial adjustment' chapter in *Editing in ArcMap*.

Exercise 10: Creating and editing annotation

Annotation is a way to store text to place on your maps. With annotation, each piece of text stores its own position, text string, and display properties. Dynamic labels, based on one or more attributes of features, are the other primary option for placing text on maps. If the exact position of each piece of text is important to you, then you should store your text as annotation. ArcGIS fully supports two types of annotation: geodatabase annotation and map document annotation. ArcGIS also supports the display and conversion of other annotation types including ArcInfo coverage annotation and CAD annotation.

In this exercise you will convert some labels into geodatabase annotation, place some unplaced annotation features, and edit some annotation features.

Opening the exercise document

1. Start ArcMap.

2. Click File and click Open. Navigate to and open the EditingAnno.mxd map document located in the Editor folder where you installed the tutorial data (C:\ArcGIS\ArcTutor is the default location).

This map shows roads and water features in Zion National Park. Each feature layer has dynamic labels, and the Streams, Major Roads, and Water Points layers have label classes based on the layers' symbology. Label classes let you create different labels for different types of features in a given layer, so, for example, intermittent streams can be given smaller labels than perennial streams.

Suppose you need to create an 8.5 x 11 inch map that shows the named streams within the park. It is more

important to get the perennial streams labeled than the intermittent ones, but your objective is to include as many stream names as possible for the park area.

Viewing unplaced labels

Some of the streams could not be labeled, due to space constraints on the map. You'll add the Labeling toolbar and view the unplaced labels.

1. Click View, point to Toolbars, and click Labeling.

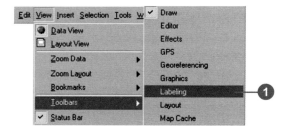

2. Click the View Unplaced Labels button.

The labels that could not be placed are displayed in red.

It might be possible to fit these labels by adjusting the size of the labels, changing the feature and label weights, or making the map larger. However, for this exercise you will convert the labels to annotation and place or delete the unplaced annotation.

3. Click the View Unplaced Labels button again, to hide the unplaced labels.

Next you'll prepare to convert the labels to annotation.

Setting a reference scale

Annotation features have a fixed position and size, so when you zoom in to the map they appear to get larger. Labels are dynamically drawn according to their layer's label properties. If the map does not have a reference scale they are drawn at their specified font size regardless of the map scale. To make labels behave more like annotation, you can set a reference scale for the map. The labels will be drawn with their specified font size scaled relative to the reference scale. When converting labels to annotation you should specify a reference scale. If you do not, the current map scale will be used as the reference scale for the annotation.

1. Type "170000" in the Map Scale box and press the Enter key.

2. In the ArcMap table of contents, right-click Layers, point to Reference Scale, and click Set Reference Scale.

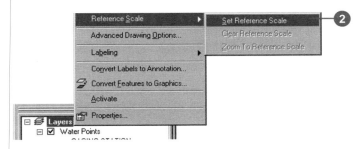

You can also view and change the reference scale for the data frame using the General tab of the Data Frame Properties dialog box.

Now if you zoom in or out, the labels will become correspondingly larger or smaller. You're ready to convert these labels to annotation.

Converting labels to annotation

Annotation can be stored in a map document or in feature classes in a geodatabase. You will convert these labels into annotation stored in a geodatabase.

1. In the ArcMap table of contents, right-click Layers and click Convert Labels to Annotation.

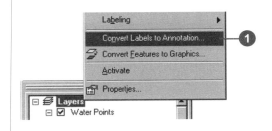

The Convert Labels to Annotation dialog box allows you to specify what kind of annotation to create from the labels, which features to create annotation for, and where the annotation will be stored.

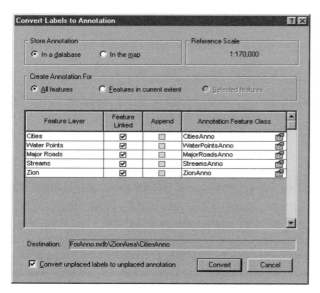

Convert Labels to Annotation dialog box with an ArcEditor or ArcInfo license of ArcMap. Annotation will be feature-linked by default.

ArcView licensed seats of ArcMap can view feature-linked annotation, but they cannot create it or edit datasets that contain it, so if you have an ArcView license the Feature Linked column of check boxes will be unavailable. For more information about feature-linked annotation, see *Building a Geodatabase*. In this exercise you will create standard annotation features. Skip the next step if you have an ArcView license.

2. Uncheck the check boxes in the Feature Linked column.

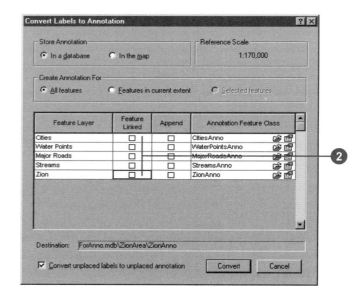

Small folder icons, the Browse buttons, appear beside the annotation feature class names as you uncheck the Feature Linked check boxes. Feature-linked annotation must be stored with the feature class that it is related to in the geodatabase. Standard annotation feature classes can be stored in other geodatabases, so after unchecking the boxes you have the option to specify a new location for your annotation. Standard annotation feature classes will be stored in the same dataset as their source feature class by default. If a feature layer on the map was based on a shapefile or coverage feature class, the Browse button would have been visible and you would need to browse to a geodatabase to store the new annotation feature class.

3. Verify that the box to Convert unplaced labels to unplaced annotation is checked.

This will give you a chance to manually place the annotation for the features that could not be labeled.

4. Click Convert.

The labels are converted to annotation. The process should take less than a minute to finish, though the speed will depend on your computer. When the annotation feature classes are created, they are added to ArcMap.

If you do this exercise with an ArcEditor or ArcInfo licensed seat of ArcMap, each layer's label classes will be stored as separate annotation classes within a single annotation feature class. For example, the two label classes

for streams will become two annotation classes, called Intermittent and Perennial, within the StreamsAnno annotation feature class. These annotation classes can be turned on and off independently, and they can have their own visible scale ranges. Annotation with multiple annotation classes can be viewed but not edited in ArcView.

If you do this exercise with an ArcView licensed seat of ArcMap, each layer's labels will be converted into a single annotation class, regardless of the number of label classes the layer has. If a layer has multiple label classes with different text symbols, each text symbol from the label classes will be available when you edit the features in the annotation class.

Preparing to place unplaced annotation

Now that the labels have been created, you will add the Editor and Annotation toolbars, switch to data view in ArcMap, and start an edit session.

1. If the Annotation toolbar is not visible, click View, point to Toolbars, and click Annotation. If the Editor toolbar is not visible, add it using the same method.

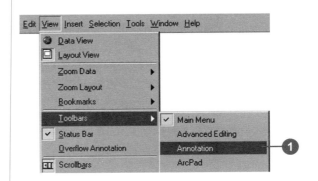

While you can edit in layout view, the display performance is better in data view.

2. Click View and click Data View.

3. Click Editor and click Start Editing.

4. Click the Unplaced Annotation Window button on the Annotation toolbar.

The Unplaced Annotation Window appears. You can resize it, dock it to the ArcMap window, or leave it floating.

The Unplaced Annotation Window lets you view unplaced annotation features in a table that can show all of the unplaced annotation in the annotation feature classes on your map. You can filter the table to show annotation for a specific annotation class and choose whether to show annotation for the whole extent of the data or for the current visible extent. You can sort the table alphabetically by the unplaced annotation's text content or annotation class by clicking the Text or Class column headings.

5. Check the Draw check box.

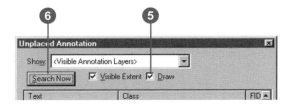

The Draw check box lets you view the unplaced annotation features on the map.

6. Click Search Now.

A number of annotation features are listed in the table. If you scroll down the table you can see that there are unplaced annotation features from several annotation classes represented.

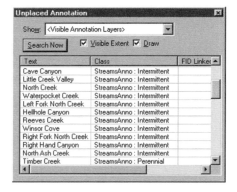

You can also see some new annotation features outlined in red on the map. You see these unplaced annotation features because the Draw check box is checked.

7. Click the Edit Annotation tool.

8. Click on the map, press and hold the Z key, and click and drag a box around the small cluster of unplaced annotation features at the east side of the park.

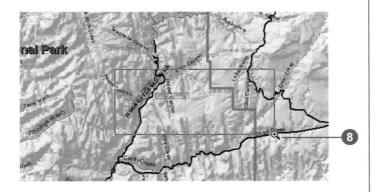

The Z key is the editing shortcut key to zoom in.

The Hillshade background layer has a visible scale range, so when you zoom in closer than 1:85,000 it is no longer displayed. Setting a visible scale range is also a good idea for annotation feature classes, as they are most useful within the range of scales where they are legible. There is no need to spend time or—especially for multiuser geodatabases—network and database resources drawing annotation features when they cannot be read. You can set a visible scale range for a layer in ArcMap, or you can change the properties of the annotation feature class itself

in ArcCatalog. The second method has the advantage that the annotation feature class will always be drawn within its visible scale range when it is added to a map.

Placing an unplaced annotation feature

Now that you've zoomed in to the cluster of unplaced annotation in the east side of the park, you're ready to start placing the unplaced annotation features.

1. Click Search Now.

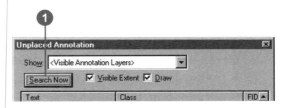

2. Right-click Cave Canyon in the Text column and click Place Annotation.

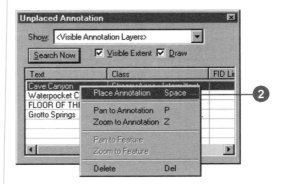

The Cave Canyon annotation feature is placed. It is selected, so it has a blue outline instead of a red outline.

The annotation feature is straight and placed parallel to a segment of the stream feature. The other stream annotation features curve to follow the streams, so you will make this newly placed annotation feature follow the stream.

Following a feature

You can make an ann~~otation feature~~ ~~fo~~llow a line feature or the boundary of a po~~lygon~~ Options dialog box ~~and~~ will behave when it ~~follows~~

1. Right-click the C~~ave Canyon~~ Follow, and clic~~k~~

   The Follow Fea~~ture~~

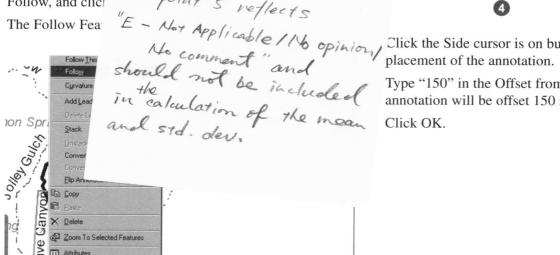

2. Click Curved.

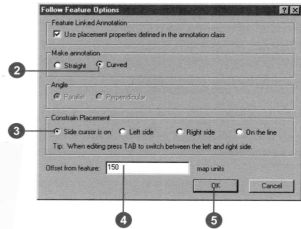

Click the Side cursor is on button to constrain the placement of the annotation.

Type "150" in the Offset from feature text box. The annotation will be offset 150 meters from the stream.

Click OK.

The way that this mean is calculated is problematic. The point 5 reflects "E – Not Applicable / No opinion / No comment" and should not be included in the calculation of the mean and std. dev.

6. Move the pointer over the stream feature just east of the Cave Canyon annotation feature. With the pointer slightly to the left of the stream, right-click and click Follow This Feature.

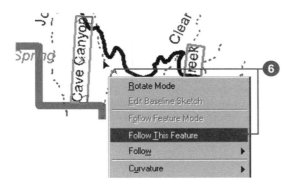

The stream feature will flash, and the annotation feature will bend to follow the stream. If you click too near the road feature, the annotation may follow the road. While the Cave Canyon annotation feature is still selected, you can fix this by repeating the last step. The selected annotation feature will follow any line feature that you right-click and tell it to follow using the Edit Annotation tool.

7. Place the pointer over the middle of the Cave Canyon annotation feature. The pointer will change to the four-pointed Move Annotation pointer.

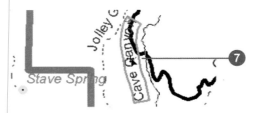

8. Click and drag the Cave Canyon annotation feature along the stream feature until it is between the park boundary and the road. It will slightly overlap each of these features. Press the L key as you drag the annotation to flip its reading direction.

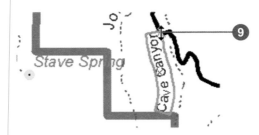

9. Place the pointer over the red triangle on the edge of the Cave Canyon annotation feature. The pointer will change to the two-pointed Resize Annotation pointer.

10. Click and drag the resize handle toward the middle of the annotation feature. The feature will shrink as you drag it. Resize the feature until it fits between the park boundary and the road.

You've placed an annotation feature, made it follow another feature, and resized it with the Edit Annotation tool. The Edit Annotation tool also allows you to make other edits to annotation features.

Stacking and rotating annotation

Now that you've placed the annotation feature from the StreamsAnno feature class, you'll place the other nearby annotation features.

1. In the Unplaced Annotation window, right-click Grotto Springs and click Pan to Annotation.

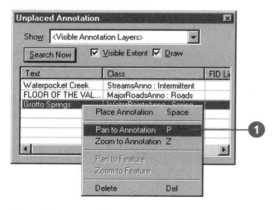

2. Press the spacebar.

   The Grotto Springs annotation feature is placed.

   The spacebar is the Unplaced Annotation window shortcut key to place a selected annotation feature.

3. Right-click the map and click Stack.

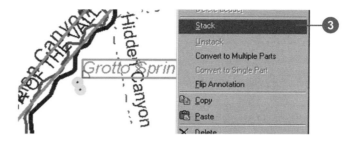

The Grotto Springs annotation feature is split at the space in the text, and the word Grotto is placed above the word Springs.

4. Move the pointer over the middle of the Grotto Springs annotation feature. The pointer will change to the four-pointed Move Annotation pointer. Click the middle of the Grotto Springs annotation feature and drag it to the southwest, so it does not cover the Hidden Canyon annotation feature.

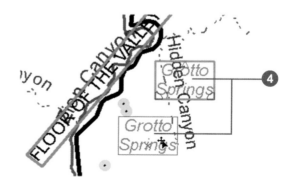

5. In the Unplaced Annotation window, click FLOOR OF THE VALLEY RD, and press the P key.

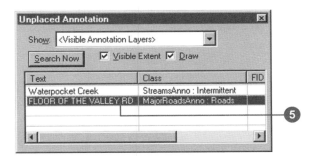

The P key is the Unplaced Annotation window shortcut key to pan to a selected annotation feature.

6. Click the map, press and hold the X key, and click and drag a box around the unplaced FLOOR OF THE VALLEY RD annotation feature.

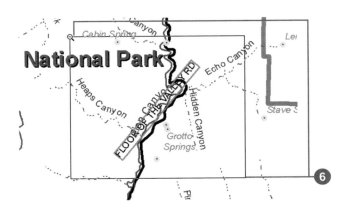

The X key is the editing shortcut key to zoom out.

7. Right-click FLOOR OF THE VALLEY RD and click Place Annotation.

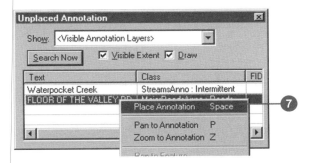

8. Click the middle of the FLOOR OF THE VALLEY RD annotation feature with the four-pointed Move Annotation pointer, and drag it to the southwest, until the south end of the annotation feature is near the intersection of Floor of the Valley Rd and the road that branches off to the east, State Highway 9.

9. Move the pointer over the blue, wedge-shaped rotate handle on the northeast corner of the FLOOR OF THE VALLEY RD annotation feature until the pointer becomes the Rotate pointer. Click the corner and drag it counter-clockwise until the annotation feature follows the general trend of the road.

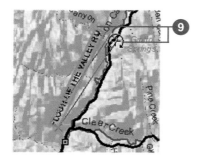

10. Right-click the FLOOR OF THE VALLEY RD annotation feature and click Stack.

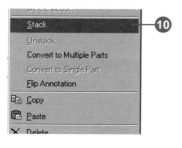

You've placed, moved, stacked, and rotated annotation features with the Edit Annotation tool. Next you'll create new annotation and delete annotation.

Creating and deleting annotation

Suppose you decide that the intersection of Floor of the Valley Rd and State Highway 9 is inadequately annotated. You'll create a new annotation feature for State Highway 9 and place it near the intersection.

1. On the Editor toolbar, click the Sketch tool.

When the Edit Annotation tool is active, you can press the E key to quickly switch between Sketch, Edit, and Edit Annotation tools.

2. Verify that the Task dropdown list says Create New Feature. If necessary, click the dropdown arrow and click Create New Feature.

3. Click the Target dropdown list and point to MajorRoadsAnno. If you are using an ArcEditor or ArcInfo license, you will have the option to choose an annotation class. Click the plus sign to expand Major RoadsAnno and click Roads. If you are using an ArcView license, click MajorRoadsAnno.

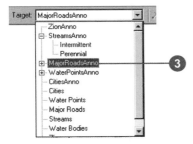

4. If you are using an ArcView license, click the Symbol dropdown list on the Annotation toolbar and click the Roads 2 symbol. If you are using an ArcEditor or ArcInfo license, the symbol will have switched to Roads 2 when you made the Roads annotation class the target for your edits.

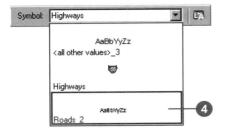

5. Press the Esc key to return focus to the Sketch tool.

When you click the dropdown lists, the Sketch tool loses focus. Pressing the Esc key returns focus to the tool so the shortcut key you will use in the next step will work.

6. Move the pointer over the road feature that branches off to the east from the intersection with Floor of the Valley Rd. Press Ctrl+W.

The Ctrl+W shortcut takes the label expression of the first visible and selectable feature that you are pointing at and adds it to the Text box on the Annotation toolbar. When you use Ctrl+W while editing a feature-linked annotation class, it uses the expression of the annotation class to derive the text and will only derive the text from a feature in the linked feature class.

The Text box on the Annotation toolbar should say STATE HWY 9. If it says ZION NATIONAL PARK or Clear Creek, move the pointer over the road feature and press Ctrl+W again.

7. Click above the road to place the new annotation feature.

Because the construction method was Horizontal, one click placed the annotation feature.

The pointer is still in Construct feature mode, and it says STATE HWY 9. If you needed to annotate more features, you could click somewhere else on the map to add another piece of annotation with the same text, or you could move the pointer over another feature and press Ctrl+W to pick up new text from its label expression. You could also type new text directly into the Text box on the Annotation toolbar. In Construct feature mode the A key is a shortcut that lets you set the focus to the Text box, so you can type new text without having to click in the box.

Most of the road annotation follows the road features. You'll use a different construction method to create a new annotation feature that follows the road.

8. Click the Construction dropdown list and click Follow Feature.

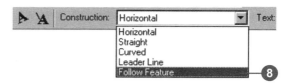

9. Click the road feature, then move the pointer along the road. The road should be highlighted, and the annotation feature should move along the road as you move the pointer. Click again to finish the annotation sketch.

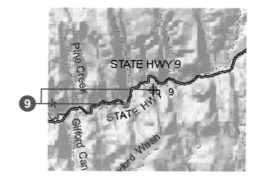

10. Press the E key to switch to the Edit tool pointer.

11. Click the horizontal STATE HWY 9 annotation feature that you created and press the Delete key.

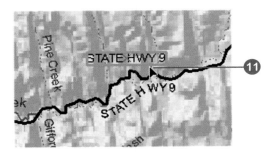

The horizontal annotation feature is deleted.

You could continue to place the unplaced annotation, edit annotation, create new annotation features, and delete unwanted annotation until the map suits your needs. This annotation is stored in geodatabase annotation feature classes, each of which can be reused on other maps.

12. Click Editor and click Save Edits, then click Editor and click Stop Editing.

In this exercise you created annotation from labels with multiple label classes, placed annotation features derived from labels that did not fit on the map, stacked and rotated annotation using the Edit Annotation tool, resized annotation features, made existing and new annotation features follow a given linear feature, and set the text string for a new annotation feature.

To learn more about editing annotation features, see 'Editing annotation' in *Editing in ArcMap*. To learn more about managing and creating geodatabase annotation feature classes, see 'Managing annotation' in *Building a Geodatabase*.

Labels can also be converted into annotation stored in a map document. Map document annotation consists of graphic and text elements rather than geodatabase features, so it is edited with the tools on the Draw toolbar. To learn more about managing and creating map document annotation, see 'Working with graphics and text' in *Using ArcMap*.

In the first two exercises, you learned how to use the edit sketch and sketch tools to create new features. There are a lot of additional methods for creating features that were not touched upon in these exercises. To learn about more ways to create new features, see the 'Creating new features' chapter in *Editing in ArcMap*.

In addition to digitizing new features using the mouse, you learned how to use a digitizer puck and tablet to capture data from paper maps. Exercise 3 showed how you can attach a paper map to your digitizing tablet, register the paper map to the coordinate space of your GIS database, and add features using the puck. To learn more about using a digitizing tablet, see the 'Using a digitizer' chapter in *Editing in ArcMap*.

In Exercise 4, you learned how easy it is to modify the shape of existing features. You copied and pasted buildings from a CAD file into your GIS database; you also moved, rotated, and scaled the buildings to match a parcel subdivision using some of the editing tools in ArcMap. Once the buildings were properly placed, you used the Extend/Trim and Modify Feature edit tasks to connect water service lines to the side of each building. To learn more about editing features in ArcMap, see the 'Editing existing features' chapter in *Editing in ArcMap*.

You can edit multiple features at the same time in ArcMap and ensure that the boundaries between them are consistent. In Exercise 5, you learned how to create a map topology and use the Topology Edit tool and two basic editing tools to edit several features at once while maintaining contiguity along their shared edge. To learn more about editing with a map topology, see the 'Editing topology' chapter in *Editing in ArcMap*.

In Exercise 6, you learned how to update your existing data with features in a CAD drawing file using the Load Objects wizard. You defined a query based on the lot line CAD layer type and loaded only those features into your target layer.

Whether importing CAD data, using a digitizer to capture features from paper, or editing the shared boundaries between polygon features, ArcMap provides the tools you need to edit your data quickly and easily.

In Exercise 7, you learned how to use a geodatabase topology and the topology error management tools in ArcMap to clean up data and create new features. To learn more about editing a geodatabase topology, see the 'Editing topology' chapter in *Editing in ArcMap*.

In Exercise 8, you learned how to use the Spatial Adjustment tool to transform, rubbersheet, and edgematch data. You created displacement links to define the source and destination locations and set adjustment properties.

In Exercise 9, you learned how to use the Spatial Adjustment tool to transfer the attributes from one feature to another. To learn more about performing spatial adjustments on your data, see the 'Spatial adjustment' chapter in *Editing in ArcMap*.

In Exercise 10, you learned how to convert labels to annotation in a geodatabase, place unplaced annotation, and edit annotation features. To learn more about editing annotation, see the 'Editing annotation' chapter in *Editing in ArcMap*. To learn more about managing and creating geodatabase annotation feature classes, see the 'Managing annotation' chapter in *Building a Geodatabase*.

Building geodatabases

4

IN THIS CHAPTER

- **Exercise 1: Organizing your data in ArcCatalog**

- **Exercise 2: Importing data into your geodatabase**

- **Exercise 3: Creating subtypes and attribute domains**

- **Exercise 4: Creating relationships between objects**

- **Exercise 5: Building a geometric network**

- **Exercise 6: Creating annotation**

- **Exercise 7: Creating layers for your geodatabase data**

- **Exercise 8: Creating a topology**

- **Exercise 9: Loading coverage data into a geodatabase topology**

It is easy to create a *geodatabase* and add *behavior* to it, and it requires no programming when you use the data management tools in ArcCatalog—the application for browsing, storing, organizing, and distributing data. When querying and editing the geodatabase in ArcMap—the application for editing, analyzing, and creating maps from your data—you can easily take advantage of the data and behavior in your geodatabase without any customization.

This tutorial lets you explore the capabilities of the geodatabase using an ArcEditor or ArcInfo licensed seat of ArcCatalog and ArcMap. You can complete this tutorial at your own pace without the need for additional assistance. This tutorial includes nine exercises. Each exercise takes between 10 and 20 minutes to complete.

In the first eight exercises of this tutorial, you will use ArcCatalog to create a geodatabase that models a water utility network. You will add behavior to the geodatabase by creating *subtypes*, *validation rules*, *relationships*, and a *geometric network*. You will use ArcMap to take advantage of the behavior by editing some of the existing *features* in the geodatabase and adding some additional features.

The study area for the first eight exercises is a portion of a hypothetical city. A geodatabase that contains most of the data, a *coverage* representing water laterals, and an INFO™ table representing parcel owner data are provided with the software. You will import the coverage and INFO table into the geodatabase, then modify its properties to give it behavior.

In the last exercise, you will take coverages and import selected feature classes into a new geodatabase. The study area for the last exercise is a portion of a drainage basin in Utah.

The datasets for the first eight exercises were created by ESRI using a database schema similar to that of the city of Montgomery, Alabama. The data is wholly fictitious and has nothing to do with the actual city of Montgomery. This information may be updated, corrected, or otherwise modified without notification.

The data for the last exercise on loading coverage data into a geodatabase topology is from the National Hydrography Dataset, published by the USGS in cooperation with the EPA, Utah AGRC, and REDCON. The watershed coverage, basin_utm, was fabricated for this exercise. This information may be updated, corrected, or otherwise modified without notification.

Exercise 1: Organizing your data in ArcCatalog

Before you begin the tutorial, you must find and organize the data that you will need. This can be done using ArcCatalog.

Connecting to data

In ArcCatalog, data is accessed through folder connections. When you look in a folder connection, you can quickly see the folders and data sources it contains. You will now begin organizing your data by creating a folder connection to it.

1. Start ArcCatalog by either double-clicking a shortcut installed on your desktop or using the Programs list in your Start menu.

2. Click the Connect To Folder button and navigate to the BuildingaGeodatabase folder on the local drive where you installed the tutorial data. The default installation path is C:\arcgis\ArcTutor\BuildingaGeodatabase. Click OK to establish a folder connection.

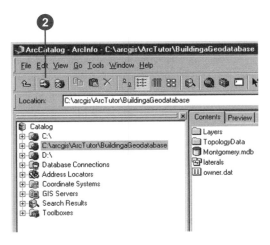

Your new folder connection— C:\arcgis\ArcTutor\BuildingaGeodatabase—is now listed in the Catalog tree. You will now be able to access all the data needed for the tutorial through that connection.

Exploring your data

Before you begin modifying the geodatabase, explore the datasets provided for the tutorial.

1. Click the plus sign next to the C:\arcgis\ArcTutor\BuildingaGeodatabase folder connection to see the datasets contained in the folder. Click the Preview tab and click the laterals coverage to see its geometry.

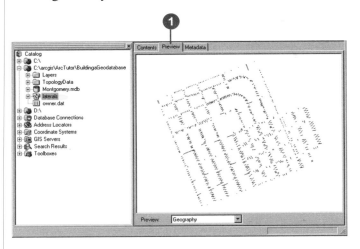

2. Click the plus sign next to the Montgomery geodatabase and double-click each *feature dataset* to see the *feature classes* and *relationship classes* it contains. Click each feature class to preview its geometry.

3. Click the owner.dat INFO *table*. Notice how the Preview type automatically changes to Table and displays the table's records. This table contains the owner information for the Parcels feature class in the Montgomery geodatabase. In the next part of this exercise, you will import this table into the geodatabase and create relationships between the parcels and their owners.

You will perform most of the tasks for modifying the Montgomery geodatabase schema with ArcCatalog. Later, you will use ArcMap to create *annotation* and edit the geodatabase.

Now that you have found and organized your data in ArcCatalog, you are ready to start the first task in the tutorial—importing data into the geodatabase.

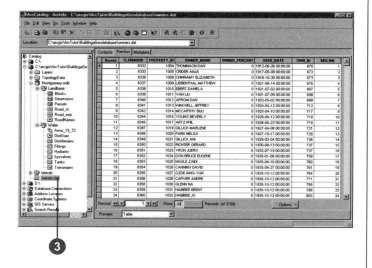

Exercise 2: Importing data into your geodatabase

Before you can start adding behavior to your data, you must get it into a geodatabase. You will import two datasets into the Montgomery geodatabase—laterals and owner.dat. The laterals coverage contains water laterals for the Montgomery water dataset, and the owner.dat INFO table contains owner information for the parcel features already in the geodatabase.

Importing the coverage

1. In ArcCatalog, right-c
   the Montgomery geod
   Feature Class (multipl

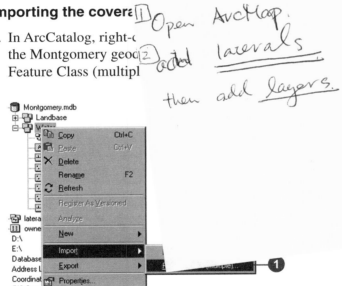

You will use the Import Feature Class tool to import the arcs in the laterals coverage into the Water feature dataset. Python must be installed on your computer for this tool to function. If you do not have Python installed, use the Import Feature Class (single) tool, which does not require Python.

This tool is used to specify your input coverage, input feature class, and output feature class. Because you opened this tool by right-clicking a feature dataset, the output geodatabase, Montgomery, and feature dataset, Water, are already filled in for you.

e are several ways to set the input and output
ets. You can also drag a dataset or datasets from the
atalog tree or Contents tab and drop them on the
ox. Alternatively, you can click the Browse button
n the ArcCatalog minibrowser and navigate to
ataset or type the full pathname to the dataset in
t box.

e Browse button, navigate to the arcs feature
the laterals coverage, and click Add.

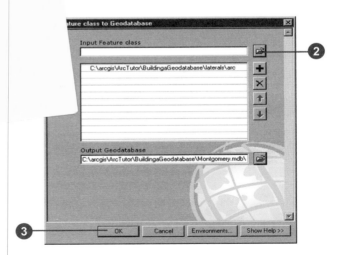

3. Click OK.

A message appears showing the progress of your data import operation. When the tool is finished, the message indicates that all the features have been imported.

The laterals_arc feature class is now in the Water feature dataset.

4. Click Close.

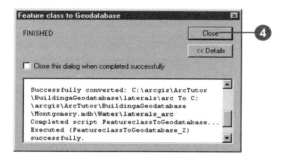

5. In the ArcCatalog tree, navigate to and click the laterals_arc feature class. Press the F2 key, and type "Laterals" to rename the feature class.

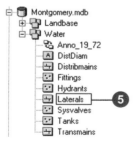

6. Click the Preview tab to see the features.

7. Right-click Laterals and click Properties.

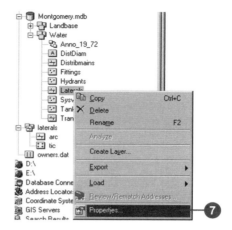

The names of feature classes and tables in a geodatabase are the same as the names of the physical tables in the relational database management system (RDBMS) in which they are stored. When you store data in an RDBMS, the names for tables and fields are often unclear, and you need a detailed data dictionary to keep track of what data each table stores and what each field in those tables represents.

The geodatabase lets you create *aliases* for *fields*, tables, and feature classes. An alias is an alternative name to refer to those items. Unlike true names, aliases can contain special characters, such as spaces, because they don't have to adhere to the database's limitations. When you use data with aliases in ArcMap, the alias name is automatically used for feature classes, tables, and fields. However, in ArcCatalog these items are always represented by their true names.

You will now create aliases for your new feature class and its fields.

8. Click the General tab.

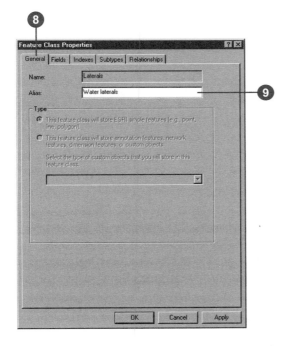

9. Type "Water laterals" for the alias for this feature class.

10. Click the Fields tab. Click the OBJECTID field and type "Feature identifier" for its alias.

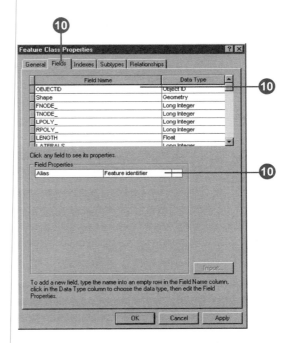

11. Repeat step 10 for the following fields:

Field	Alias
Shape	Geometry field
DEPTH_BURI	Depth buried
RECORDED_L	Recorded length
FACILITY_I	Facility identifier
DATE_INSTA	Installation date
TYPECODE	Subtype code

12. Click OK.

Now that you have imported the Laterals feature class into the geodatabase and added some aliases, you are ready to import the owner.dat INFO table.

Importing the INFO table

The owner.dat INFO table contains owner information for the parcels in the Parcels feature class in the Montgomery geodatabase. To be able to create relationships between the parcels and their owners, the owner information must be imported into the Montgomery geodatabase. You will use the Table (multiple) import tool to import the owner.dat INFO table into the Montgomery geodatabase. You will then create aliases for the table.

1. Right-click the Montgomery geodatabase, point to Import, then click Table (multiple).

2. Drag and drop the owners.dat INFO table from the Catalog tree to the Input Table box.

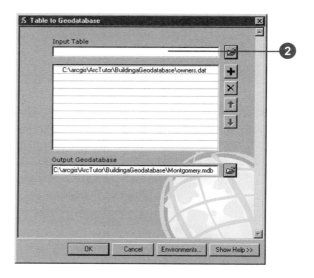

3. Click OK. A message informs you of the progress of the operation. When it finishes, click Close.

4. In the ArcCatalog tree, click the Owners table in the Montgomery geodatabase. Click the Preview tab to see its rows.

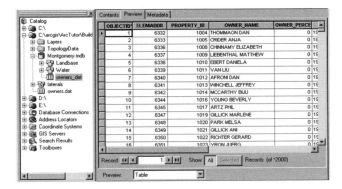

5. Press the F2 key, and type "Owners" to rename the table.

6. Right-click the Owners table and click Properties to see the table's properties.

7. Type "Parcel owners" for the alias for this table.

8. Click the Fields tab and type the following field aliases:

Field	Alias
OBJECTID	Object identifier
OWNER_NAME	Owner name
OWNER_PERCENT	Percentage ownership
DEED_DATE	Date of deed

9. Click OK.

The data in the laterals coverage and owners.dat INFO table is now in the Montgomery geodatabase. Now you can take advantage of the geodatabase by applying behavior to your data. You will begin this task by creating subtypes and *attribute domains*.

t. ~~Hay~~ Need to close the preview before changing the ~~file~~ table & name.

(181)

Exercise 3: Creating subtypes and attribute domains

One of the advantages of storing your data in a geodatabase is that you can define rules about how the data can be edited. You will define these rules by creating a new attribute domain for lateral diameters; creating subtypes for the Laterals feature class; and associating the new domain, existing domains, and default values with fields for each subtype.

Attribute domains are rules that describe the legal values of a field type. Multiple feature classes and tables can share attribute domains stored in the database. However, not all the objects in a feature class or table need to share the same attribute domains.

For example, in a water network, suppose that only hydrant water laterals can have a pressure between 40 and 100 psi, while service water laterals can have a pressure between 50 and 75 psi. You would use an attribute domain to enforce this restriction. To implement this kind of validation rule, you do not have to create separate feature classes for hydrant and service water laterals, but you would want to distinguish these types of water laterals from each other to establish a separate set of domains and default values. You can do this using subtypes.

To learn more about subtypes and attribute domains, see the chapter on subtypes and attribute domains in *Building a Geodatabase*.

Creating an attribute domain

You will use ArcCatalog to create a new coded value attribute domain. This new domain will describe a set of valid pipe diameters for your new Laterals feature class.

1. Right-click the Montgomery geodatabase and click Properties.

2. Click the Domains tab.

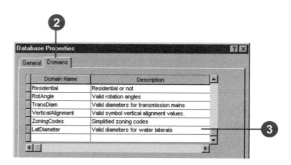

3. Click the first empty field under Domain Name and type "LatDiameter" for the name of the new domain. In the Description field, type "Valid diameters for water laterals" for the domain's description.

Y...
T... ...n.
c... ...ain
o... ...range
v... ...he
A...
v... ...c
v... ...of
v... ...ded

A... ...hen a
fe... ...olicies
to...
fe...

4. Cl... ...lick
Fl...

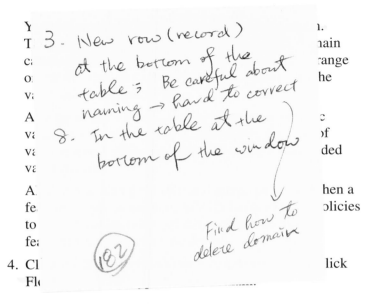

(handwritten note)
3. New row (record) at the bottom of the table; Be careful about naming → hard to correct

8. In the table at the bottom of the window

182

Find how to delete domain

5. Click the Domain Type to view a dropdown list and click Coded Values for the domain type.

6. Click the *Split policy* to view a dropdown list and click Duplicate for the split policy for the domain. The *Merge policy* will default to Default Value.

You'll type the valid values, or codes, for the coded value domain, and for each code you will provide a user-friendly description. As you will see later in the tutorial, ArcMap uses the user-friendly description, not the code, for values of fields that have coded value domains associated with them.

7. Click the first empty field under Code and type "13" for the code; then click the Description field beside it and type "13"" for the code's description.

8. Add the following coded values to the list:

Code	Description
10	10"
8	8"
6	6"
4	4"
3	3"
2.25	2 1/4"
2	2"
1.5	1 1/2"
1.25	1 1/4"
1	1"
0.75	3/4"
-9	Unknown

9. Click OK to add the domain to the geodatabase.

Creating subtypes and associating default values and domains

Now you will create subtypes for the Laterals feature class and associate default values and domains with the fields for each subtype. By creating subtypes, not all the water lateral features need to have the same domains, default values, and as you will see later in the tutorial, connectivity rules.

1. Right-click the Laterals feature class and click Properties.

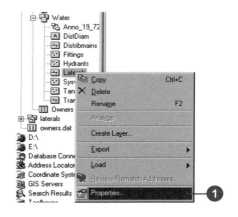

2. Click the Subtypes tab.

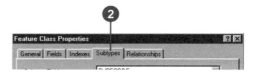

You will now specify the subtype field for the Laterals feature class. The subtype field contains the values that identify to which subtype a particular feature belongs.

3. Click the Subtype Field dropdown arrow and click TYPECODE.

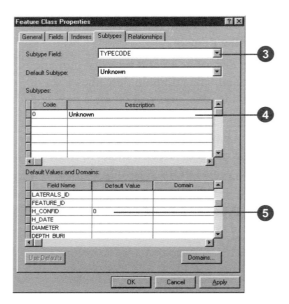

You will now add subtype codes and their descriptions. When you add a new subtype, you will assign default values and domains to some of its fields.

4. Click the Description field next to subtype code 0 and type "Unknown" for its description.

5. Click the Default Value field next to **H_CONFID** and type "0" for its default value. Do the same for **DEPTH_BURI** and **RECORDED_L**. For the **WNM_TYPE**, **PWTYPE** fields, type "WUNKNOWN" as the default values.

6. Click the Default Value field next to **DIAMETER** and type "8" for the default value. Click the Domain dropdown list and click LatDiameter to set it as this field's attribute domain for the Unknown subtype.

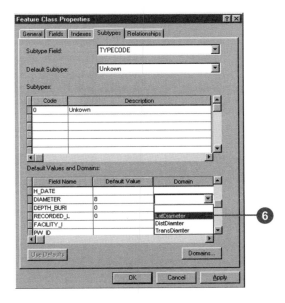

Code	Description
1	Hydrant laterals
WNM_TYPE, PWTYPE	default value = WHYDLIN
2	Fire laterals
WNM_TYPE, PWTYPE	default value = WFIRELIN
3	Service laterals
WNM_TYPE, PWTYPE	default value = WSERVICE

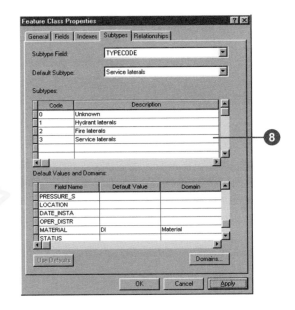

7. Repeat step 6 for the **MATERIAL** field, typing "DI" for the default value. Click Material in the Domain dropdown list.

8. Add the following subtypes and set the default values and domains the same as for the Unknown subtype, except for the WNM_TYPE and PWTYPE field default values.

When adding new features to a feature class with subtypes in the ArcMap editing environment, if you don't specify a particular subtype, the new feature will be assigned the default subtype. Once you have added all the subtypes for this feature class, you can set the default subtype from those you entered.

9. Click the Default Subtype dropdown arrow and click Service laterals to set it as the default subtype.

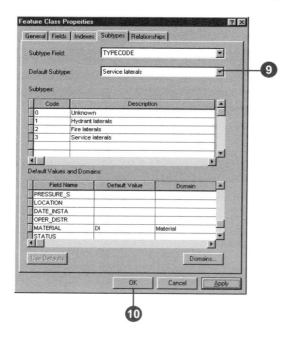

10. Click OK.

You have now added behavior to the geodatabase by adding domains and creating subtypes. Now you will add some additional behavior to the geodatabase by creating relationships.

Exercise 4: Creating relationships between objects

In Exercise 2, you imported an INFO table containing owner objects into the Montgomery geodatabase. The geodatabase already has a feature class called Parcels that contains parcel objects. You will now create a *relationship class* between the parcels and the owners so that when you use the data in ArcMap you can easily find out which owners own which parcels.

1. Right-click the Landbase feature dataset, point to New, then click Relationship Class.

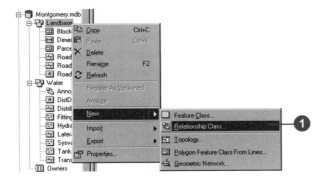

The New Relationship Class wizard opens. The first panel of the wizard is used to specify the name, origin, and destination feature class or table for the new relationship class.

2. Type "ParcelOwners" as the name of this relationship class.

3. Click Owners for the origin table.

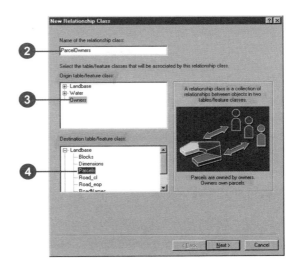

4. Double-click Landbase and click Parcels for the destination feature class. Click Next.

The next panel is used to specify the type of relationship class you are creating. You are creating a simple relationship class since owners and parcels can exist in the database independently of each other. You can, therefore, accept the default type—simple relationship class.

5. Click Next.

You must now specify the path labels and the message notification direction. The forward path label describes the relationship as it is navigated from the origin class to the destination class—in this case, from Owners to Parcels. The backward path label describes the relationship when navigated in the other direction—from Parcels to Owners.

The message notification direction describes how messages are passed between related objects. Message notification is not required for this relationship class, so accept the default of None.

6. Type "owns" for the forward path label and type "is owned by" for the backward path label. Click Next.

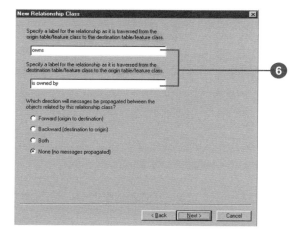

You will now specify the cardinality of the relationship. The cardinality describes the possible number of objects in the destination feature class or table that can be related to an object in the origin feature class or table.

7. Click 1–M (one-to-many) to specify that one owner may own many parcels. Click Next.

You must now specify whether your new relationship class will have attributes. In this example, the ParcelOwners relationship class does not require attributes, which is the default.

8. Click Next.

The next step is to specify the primary key in the origin table (Owners) and the embedded foreign key field in the destination feature class (Parcels). Owners and Parcels that have the same value in these fields will be related to each other.

9. Click the first dropdown arrow and click PROPERTY_ID for the origin table primary key.

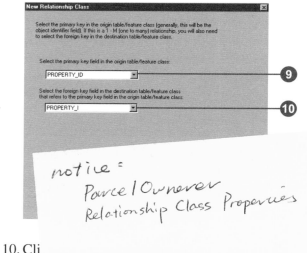

notice =
Parcel/Owner
Relationship Class Properties

10. Cli
   PR(
   desi   Remove an underscore from
11. Clic   the name
   revi

   You
   geod
   add h   ric
   netwo

Exercise 5: Building a geometric network

Feature classes stored in the same feature dataset can participate in a geometric network. Geometric networks model network systems such as water networks. You will build a geometric network from the feature classes in the Water feature dataset in the Montgomery geodatabase. You will then create connectivity rules to define which features can connect to each other in the network.

Creating the water network

1. Right-click the Water dataset, point to New, then click Geometric Network.

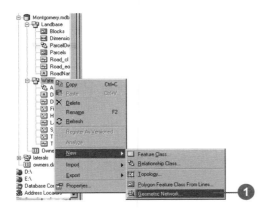

The Build Geometric Network Wizard opens. You can use this wizard to either build a geometric network from existing feature classes or to create an empty geometric network. In this case, you will be building a network from the existing feature classes in the Water feature dataset.

2. Click Next.

   The second panel is used to specify whether to build a network from existing feature classes or to create an empty one. You want the default—Build a geometric network from existing features.

3. Click Next.

   You must now select which feature classes in the feature dataset will participate in the geometric network and what the name of the network will be.

4. Click Select All.

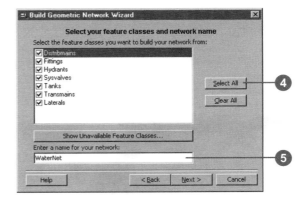

5. Type "WaterNet" for the name of the geometric network. Click Next.

The option to exclude features with certain attributes makes it easier to manage the state of parts of the network if you need to drop the network and rebuild it after you've been working with it for a while.

6. Click No, so that all features will participate in the geometric network. Click Next.

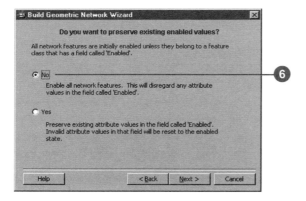

You will now specify which line feature classes will become complex edge feature classes in the geometric network. Complex edge features are not split into two features by the connection of another feature along their length; thus, they are useful for modeling water mains which may have multiple laterals connected to them. By default, all line feature classes become simple edge feature classes.

7. Click Yes to specify that some of the line feature classes will become complex edges.

8. Check Distribmains and Transmains to make the water distribution and transmission mains complex edges. Click Next.

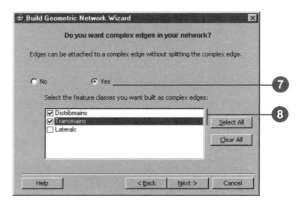

Features in a geometric network must be precisely connected to one another. The input feature classes can be adjusted to ensure connectivity by snapping. You will specify whether these features need to be adjusted to snap to one another in the network-building process.

9. Click Yes to specify that some of the features need to be adjusted. Type "1.0" for the snapping tolerance.

10. Click Select All to indicate that the features stored in each feature class can be adjusted. Click Next.

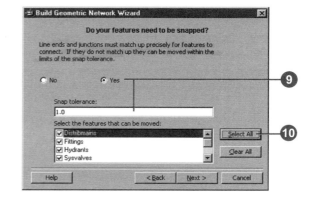

You must specify which, if any, of the junction feature classes can act as sources and sinks in the network. Sources and sinks are used to determine the flow direction in the network.

11. Click Yes to indicate that some of the junction feature classes will act as sources or sinks.

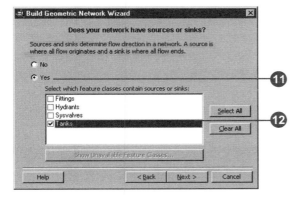

12. Check the Tanks feature class to indicate that tanks can be sources or sinks in the network. Click Next.

Now you can assign network weights. A network weight describes the cost of traversing an element in the logical network, such as the drop in pressure as water flows through a pipe. This geometric network does not require weights, which is the default.

13. Click Next. A summary page appears. Once you have reviewed the summary, click Finish.

A progress indicator appears, displaying the progress for each stage of the network-building process.

Your new geometric network, WaterNet, has been created in the Montgomery geodatabase. Next, you'll establish *connectivity rules* for your water network.

Creating connectivity rules

Network connectivity rules constrain the type of network features that may be connected to one another and the number of features of any particular type that can be connected to features of another type. By establishing these rules, you can maintain the integrity of the network connectivity in the database.

1. Right-click WaterNet and click Properties.

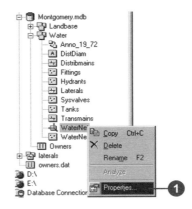

The Geometric Network Properties dialog box opens. The dialog box provides information about feature classes participating in the network and a list of the network weights. You can also add, delete, and modify connectivity rules using this dialog box.

2. Click the Connectivity tab.

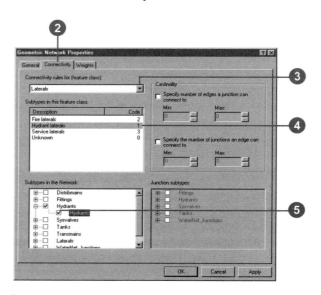

This tab lets you add and modify connectivity rules for the geometric network. You will first create a new *edge–junction rule*, which states that hydrants can connect to hydrant laterals; it also indicates that when a hydrant lateral is created, a hydrant junction feature should be placed at its free end.

3. Click the dropdown arrow and click Laterals.

4. In the list of subtypes in the feature class, click Hydrant laterals.

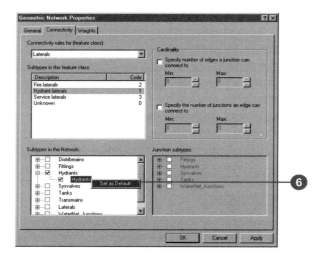

You will now click the types of junctions that hydrant laterals can connect to in the network. For simplicity, hydrant laterals can only connect to hydrants.

5. Check Hydrants in the list of subtypes in the network.

You should also specify that when you create a hydrant lateral, if an end of the lateral is not connected to another edge or junction, then a hydrant is placed at that end.

6. Click the plus sign to expand Hydrants, right-click Hydrants under it, then click Set as Default. A blue D will appear next to the hydrant subtype, indicating that it is the default junction for this edge subtype.

You will now create a new *edge–edge rule* that states that hydrant laterals can connect to distribution mains through taps, tees, and saddles. The default junction for connections between hydrant laterals and distribution mains will be taps.

7. In the network subtypes list, click the plus sign to expand Distribmains and check Distribmains under it.

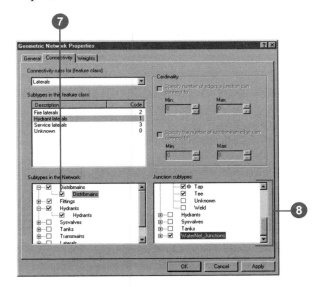

Because you have checked an edge in the network subtypes list, the list of junction subtypes in the network becomes active. In this list, you can specify which junction types hydrant laterals and distribution mains can connect through.

8. In the Junction subtypes list, click the plus sign to expand Fittings and check Tap, Tee, and Saddle in that order. Notice that Tap has a blue D next to it; this means that Tap is the *default junction*. Check WaterNet_Junctions, which is the generic, or default, network junction type.

9. Click OK.

You have now added behavior to your geodatabase by defining connectivity rules. You would normally define many more connectivity rules for a network. However, for this tutorial, you only need to define the connectivity rules specified here. In the next part of the tutorial, you will create feature-linked *annotation* for your new hydrant lateral feature class.

Exercise 6: Creating annotation

In Exercise 1, you browsed through the existing feature classes in the Montgomery geodatabase. One of these feature classes contained annotation that was linked to features in the Distribmains feature classes. You then imported the water laterals from a coverage into the Water feature dataset. Now you will create labels for the water laterals in ArcMap and convert them to an annotation feature class that is linked to the laterals.

Creating labels for the lateral subtypes

You'll start ArcMap and add the Laterals feature class.

1. Click the Launch ArcMap button. Start a new, empty map document.

2. Click the Laterals feature class, drag it from ArcCatalog, and drop it on the ArcMap table of contents.

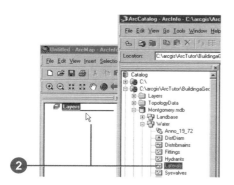

Because you created subtypes for the Laterals feature class, each subtype is automatically drawn with unique symbols. You'll create different label classes for the subtypes.

3. In ArcMap, right-click Laterals and click Properties.

4. Click the Labels tab.

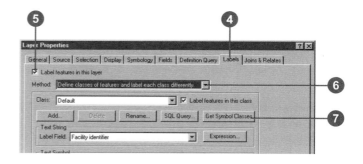

5. Check the box to Label features in this layer.

6. Click the Method dropdown list and click Define classes of features and label each class differently.

7. Click Get Symbol Classes.

Now the layer has several label classes defined—one for each subtype and one for other values.

Defining the labels for the hydrant laterals

The different subtypes of laterals have different roles in the water system. For example, service laterals bring water from the distribution mains to residences or businesses, and hydrant laterals bring water from mains to fire hydrants. You will make the labels for the hydrant laterals red to make it easy for map readers to differentiate hydrant laterals from other laterals.

1. Click the Class dropdown list and click Hydrant laterals.

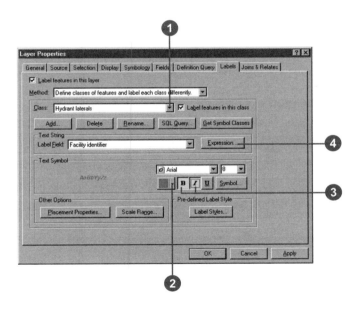

2. Click the text color dropdown arrow and click a red swatch from the palette.

3. Click the Bold and Italic buttons.

4. Click Expression.

Sometimes you want to label features with the content of a single field. The Label Field dropdown list lets you select a single field with which to label features. At other times, you may want to create more complex labels. The Label Expression dialog box lets you construct labels by concatenating one or more fields and other text. You can also add logic to the label expression using a scripting language.

To create the labels for the hydrant laterals, you'll load a label expression that has been saved to a file.

5. Click Load.

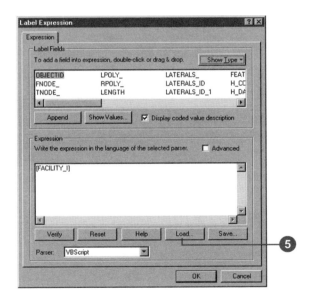

The label expression has been saved to a file called "lateral_exp.lxp" in the Layers folder for the BuildingAGeodatabase tutorial folder.

6. Navigate to the Layers folder, click lateral_exp.lxp, and click Open.

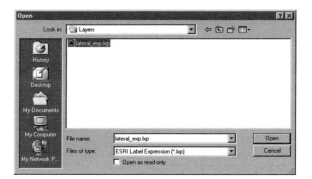

This VBScript expression evaluates the length of each lateral; if its value is greater than 200, it labels the lateral with the contents of the DIAMETER field, a space, and the contents of the MATERIAL field. If the length is less than 200, it labels the lateral with the contents of the DIAMETER field.

You will adjust this expression for the Hydrant laterals so that Hydrant laterals longer than 100 feet get the more complete labels.

7. Click in the Expression box and change the value in the If statement from 200 to 100. Click Verify.

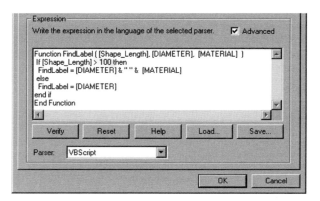

The expression is tested and a sample is displayed.

8. Click OK on the Label Expression Verification dialog box and click OK on the Label Expression dialog box.

You've created an expression for the Hydrant laterals label class. Next you'll create expressions for the label classes of the other subtypes.

Defining the labels for the service laterals

The service laterals tend to be shorter than the hydrant laterals. For this exercise, it is only important to show their material type when they are longer than 200 feet, so you will load the label expression again and use it without modifying it.

1. Click the Class dropdown list and click Service laterals.

   Now you can set up the label parameters for this label class.

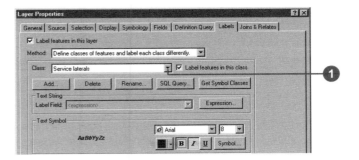

2. Use the same procedure that you just used to define the labels for the Hydrant laterals, but make these labels black, and do not modify the label expression after you load it.

Defining the labels for other laterals

You've loaded label expressions for the Hydrant laterals and Service laterals. Now you'll define the labels for Fire laterals, Unknown laterals, and the <all other values> class. Because these classes are less common and only the diameter is of interest, you will use the Diameter field alone to label these features.

1. Click the Class dropdown list and click Fire laterals.

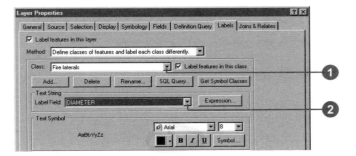

2. Click the Label Field dropdown list and click DIAMETER.

3. Use the same procedure to set the labels for the Unknown and <all other values> label classes.

4. Click OK on the Layer Properties dialog box.

   The labels are drawn on the map. The Hydrant laterals are labeled in red, and because of the label expression, the longer ones are also labeled with their material type.

You've created labels for the different subtypes of laterals, using the symbology classes in ArcMap to derive the label classes. Now you will convert the labels to annotation in the geodatabase.

Setting the reference scale for the labels

Labels are dynamic—they are regenerated when you pan and zoom around the map. By default, they will be drawn using the same size symbol, regardless of the scale to which you zoom. Not all features can be labeled using an 8 point font at the full extent of the feature class, but if you zoom in, there will be more space around the features, so more labels will be drawn.

Unlike labels, annotation is static. Annotation features are stored. They have a fixed location and a reference scale, so when you zoom in, the text gets larger on the screen.

You can make labels behave more like annotation by setting a reference scale. This should be the scale at which the map will most commonly be used. When you convert the labels to annotation, you want the annotation to have the right reference scale so it will be drawn at the right size, relative to the features, on the maps you create.

1. Click the Zoom In tool and click and drag a box around some of the laterals on the eastern edge of the data.

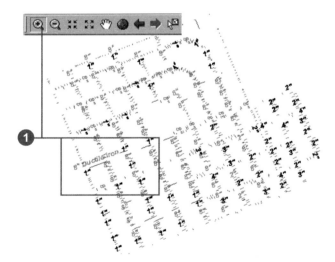

Labels are now drawn for more of the laterals.

2. Type 1000 in the Scale box and press Enter.

Even more of the labels are now drawn. This is the scale at which the data will usually be drawn, so you will now set the reference scale for the map and the annotation that you create from it.

3. Right-click Layers, point to Reference Scale, and click Set Reference Scale.

Now, when you zoom in or out, the labels will get larger or smaller.

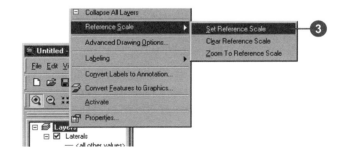

Converting the labels to annotation

Now that the reference scale is set, you can convert the labels to annotation and store them in your geodatabase. You will convert the label classes into subtypes of a single feature-linked annotation feature class. This process requires an ArcEditor or ArcInfo licensed seat of ArcMap. With an ArcView seat, you can create annotation from labels but not feature-linked annotation or annotation feature classes with multiple annotation classes.

1. Right-click Layers and click Convert Labels to Annotation.

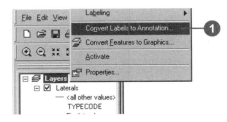

2. Click the Properties button.

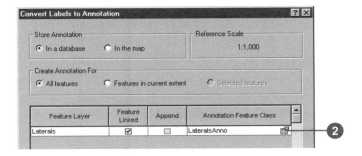

3. Check the box to Require symbol to be selected from the symbol table.

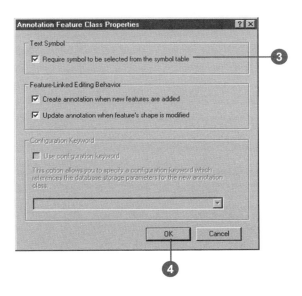

This will reduce the storage space needed in the geodatabase for the annotation. Each annotation feature will reference a symbology table in the geodatabase, rather than storing all its own symbology information. You will not be able to store graphics in this annotation feature class.

The check boxes for the two feature-linked annotation editing behavior options are checked by default. New annotation will be created when new laterals are added, and existing annotation will move when laterals are moved or reshaped.

4. Click OK.

5. Click Convert.

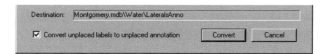

A message box will appear showing the progress of the conversion process. After a short time, it will finish.

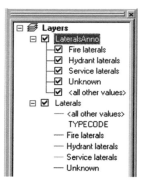

The labels are converted to a set of annotation classes within a single annotation feature class. A relationship class is also created that links the annotation to the laterals.

6. Close ArcMap.

You've created an annotation feature class in the geodatabase. The annotation classes within it correspond to the subclasses of the laterals feature class. Some of these annotation classes have special symbology, as well as logic to annotate certain features with extra information. When the Laterals feature class is edited in ArcMap, the corresponding annotation features will be created or

modified using the symbology and annotation expression you created.

Exercise 7: Creating layers for your geodatabase data

To make browsing for and symbolizing data more convenient, you can create layers from your geodatabase data and use these layers in ArcMap. Most of the layers you will need have been created for you; they are stored in the Layers folder in your tutorial directory. In this exercise, you will create new layers for the Laterals and the LateralsAnno feature classes.

Creating the Laterals layer

1. In ArcCatalog, right-click the Laterals feature class and click Create Layer.

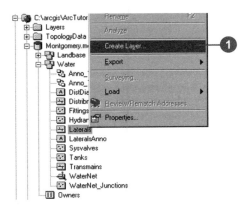

2. Browse to the Layers folder under your tutorial directory and type "Water Laterals" for the name of the new layer.

3. Click Save.

The new layer is created. You will modify the properties of the layer to add symbology.

4. Open the Layers folder in the ArcCatalog tree, right-click the Water Laterals layer, then click Properties.

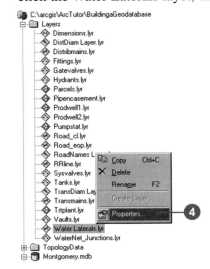

You can use the Layer Properties dialog box to modify many aspects of a layer, such as its visible scale and transparency. In this case, you will modify its symbology.

5. Click the Symbology tab.

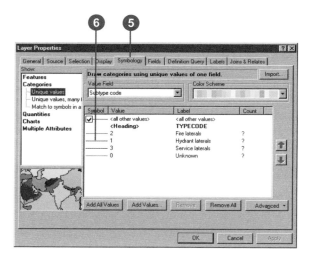

By default, the Unique values classification based on the subtype field is used to symbolize the layer. This is the setting you want, but you must modify the symbology of each subtype.

6. Double-click the colored line next to Hydrant laterals.

The Symbol Selector dialog box appears. You will use this dialog box to set the symbol properties for the laterals.

7. Click the Color dropdown arrow and click a purple patch on the color palette to make the line purple.

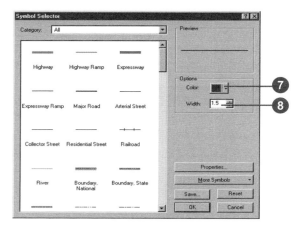

8. Type "1.5" in the width text box to give the line a width of 1.5.

9. Click OK.

10. Repeat steps 6 through 9 for the Fire laterals, making the symbol a red line with a width of 1.5.

11. Repeat steps 6 through 9 for the Service laterals, making the symbol a dark blue line with a width of 1.5.

12. Click OK to close the Properties dialog box.

Your Water Laterals layer is complete. You can now create the annotation layer for the water laterals.

Creating the LateralDiam layer

1. Right-click the LateralsAnno feature class and click Create Layer.

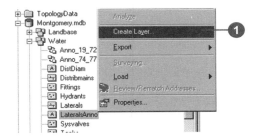

2. Navigate to the Layers folder and type "Water lateral diameter annotation" for the name of the new layer.

3. Click Save.

The new annotation layer is created. Since this layer points to an annotation feature class, the symbology is a property of the annotation, so it does not have to be set in the layer.

Setting a visible scale range for the layer

Annotation features are most useful within a fairly narrow range of map scales in which they are legible. It is often helpful to set a minimum and maximum scale within which annotation feature classes will be drawn. You can make this visible scale range a property of the annotation feature class itself or set it as a property of a layer that points to the annotation feature class. For large annotation feature classes and in multiuser environments, the former approach is best, as it is the most effective way to prevent large numbers of annotation features from being needlessly requested from the server.

For this exercise, assume that users of this feature class will usually add the layer you've created, rather than adding the annotation feature class directly.

1. In ArcCatalog, right-click Water lateral diameter annotation.lyr.

2. Click the General tab.

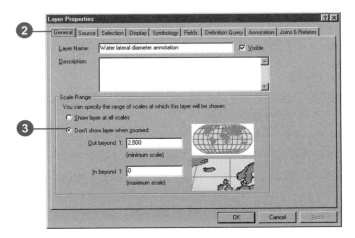

3. Click the Don't show layer when zoomed button, type "2500" in the Out beyond 1 box, and click OK.

To set the scale range for an annotation feature class, right-click the annotation feature class in ArcCatalog, click Properties, and click the Annotation Classes tab. You can set a separate scale range for each annotation class in the annotation feature class. Click the Scale Range button to set the minimum and maximum visible scales.

You have successfully imported coverage and INFO data into your geodatabase and created subtypes, rules, a geometric network, and feature-linked annotation. Now you will create a topology.

Exercise 8: Creating a topology

In Exercise 5, you created a geometric network. A geometric network is a specialized type of topological relationship that allows network tracing, analysis, and editing. In this exercise, you will create a geodatabase topology. A geodatabase topology allows you to specify rules that control the spatial relationships of features in a dataset. There are a variety of topology rules that you can apply to your data, depending on your organization's requirements. You will only apply two topology rules to this dataset.

Creating a topology

You'll create the topology to regulate two types of spatial relationships in this dataset. The first is that parcels should not overlap, and the second is that parcels that have been classified as residential must fall within blocks that are also classified as residential.

1. Navigate to the Landbase dataset in ArcCatalog.

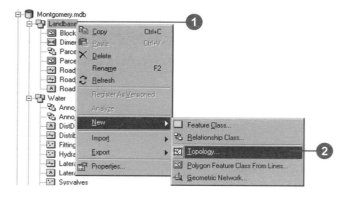

This dataset contains several feature classes. You will create a topology using two feature classes—Parcels and Blocks.

2. Right-click Landbase, point to New, then click Topology.

The New Topology wizard starts. The first page provides a brief description of the wizard.

3. Click Next.

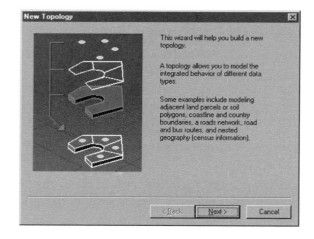

The wizard presents a default name and cluster tolerance for the topology.

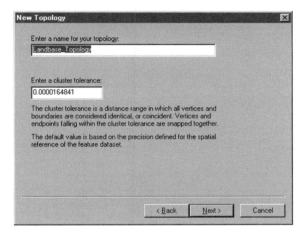

The cluster tolerance is based on the precision of the Landbase dataset's spatial reference. This dataset has a limited geographic extent, with an east–west coordinate range of 498,461–515,641 feet and a north–south coordinate range of 674,377–691,556 feet, or about 3.25 miles in each direction. Because of its limited extent, the dataset can support a very high precision: 124,999 of the 2.14 billion available geodatabase storage units per spatial reference linear unit. The linear units are feet, so this dataset can store—within this small area—differences in position as small as 8×10^{-6} feet. The default cluster tolerance will make parts of features within 1.6×10^{-5} feet of each other snap together.

You will accept the default name and cluster tolerance that the wizard provides.

4. Click Next.

5. Check Blocks and Parcels.

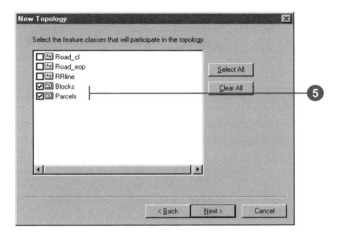

These feature classes will participate in the topology.

One of the topology rules that you'll create will concern the Parcels feature class, and the other will be between one subtype of Parcels and one subtype of Blocks, so both Blocks and Parcels feature classes must participate in the topology. If one of these feature classes were already participating in another topology or a geometric network or if they were registered as versioned in a multiuser geodatabase, it would not appear in the list of feature classes available to add to this topology.

6. Click Next.

The next page of the wizard allows you to set the number of topology ranks and the rank of each feature class in the topology.

Ranks allow you to ensure that more accurately collected features are not snapped to the position of less accurately collected ones when the topology is validated. For example, if you were including a feature class that was collected using a survey grade global positioning system (GPS) unit and a feature class digitized from a 1:1,000,000-scale source map in the same topology, you might assign the GPS feature class a rank of 1 and the 1:1,000,000-scale source feature class a rank of 5. If you were to validate the topology, parts of features that fell within the cluster tolerance would snap together, with the less accurate ones moving to the location of the more accurate ones. The GPS features would not be moved to the position of the 1:1,000,000-scale features.

You can assign up to 50 different ranks, with 1 being the highest rank. In this topology, you will assume that all the feature classes are based on equally accurate data, so you will not assign more than one rank. Parcels and Blocks have equivalent levels of accuracy, since the Blocks feature class was derived from the parcel features.

7. Type "1" for the number of ranks.

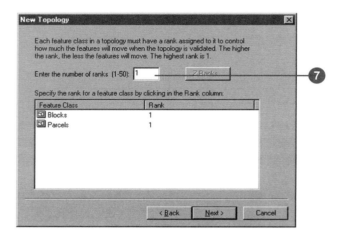

8. Click Next.

9. Click Add Rule.

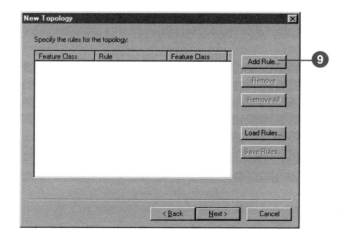

Topology rules allow you to define the permissible spatial relationships of features within and between feature classes that participate in the topology.

Landownership parcels are usually not allowed to overlap each other. You will add a rule to prevent your parcel features from overlapping each other.

10. Click the Features of feature class dropdown arrow and click Parcels.

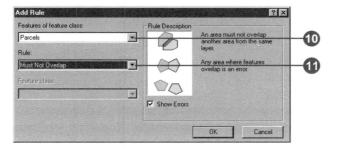

11. Click the Rule dropdown arrow and click Must Not Overlap.

12. Click OK.

You've created a rule governing the topological relationship of features within the same feature class. Next you'll create a topology rule governing the topological relationship of features in particular subtypes of two different feature classes. Specifically, you'll make sure that residential parcels are covered by or contained within blocks also designated as residential.

13. Click Add Rule.

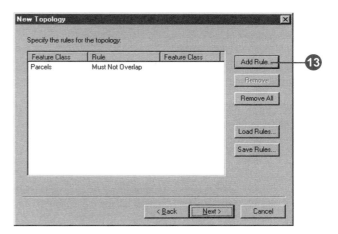

14. Click the Features of feature class dropdown arrow, click the plus sign to expand Parcels, and click Residential.

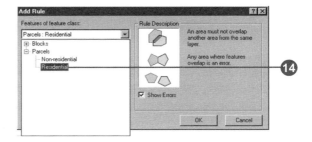

Residential is a subtype of the Parcels feature class that the planning department uses to represent parcels where people live.

15. Click the Rule dropdown arrow and click Must Be Covered By.

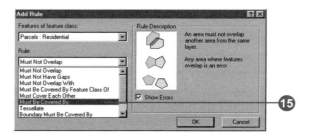

16. Click the Feature class dropdown arrow, click the plus sign to expand Blocks, and click Residential.

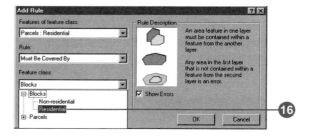

17. Click OK.

The topology rule is added to the list of rules for this topology.

18. Click Next.

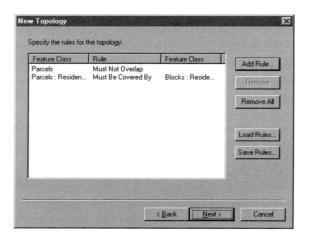

19. Click Finish.

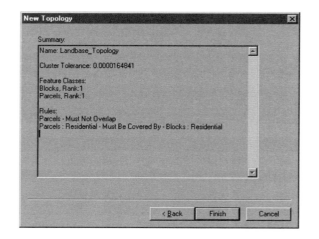

After the topology is created, you have the opportunity to validate it. You do not need to validate the topology immediately after creating it. Depending on your data and your work flow, it may make sense to assign different areas to data editors to validate and edit within ArcMap.

20. Click No.

The topology appears in the Landbase dataset.

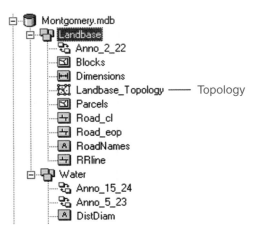

Exercise 9: Loading coverage data into a geodatabase topology

Imagine you manage water resources for a county. You want to create a geodatabase from existing data in coverages. You will import the relevant feature classes from a group of coverages for a reservoir; its flood stage inundation area; and contributing streams, as well as ponds, wells, and springs, within the watershed. You will then add topology rules that would be useful for managing this data.

Navigating to the data and creating a geodatabase

First, you'll find the existing data and create a geodatabase.

1. Navigate to the TopologyData folder in the BuildingaGeodatabase folder.

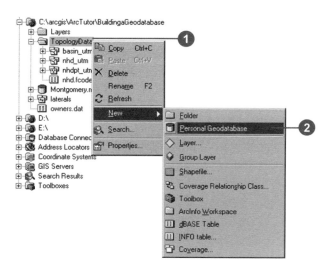

2. Right-click TopologyData, point to New, then click Personal Geodatabase.

   A new personal geodatabase is created in the TopologyData folder. The temporary name, New Personal Geodatabase, is selected so you can easily rename it.

3. Type "CountyWater" and press the Enter key to rename the geodatabase.

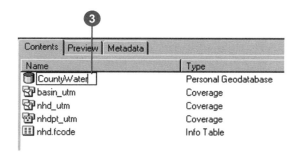

You will be creating a topology to control the spatial relationships between some of the features and feature classes. Feature classes that participate in a topology must have the same spatial reference, so they must be in the same feature dataset. Since this geodatabase does not contain a feature dataset, you will create one.

Creating a new feature dataset

Geodatabase feature datasets can contain a number of feature classes that share a spatial reference. Because the feature classes share a spatial reference, they can participate in topologies and geometric networks with other feature classes in the dataset. In this step, you will create the dataset and calculate the correct XY domain for your data.

1. Right-click the CountyWater geodatabase, point to New, then click Feature Dataset.

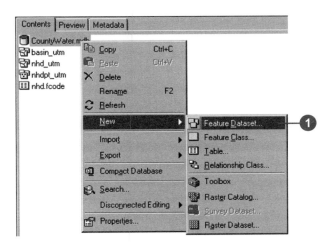

The New Feature Dataset dialog box appears. Next, you'll name the dataset.

2. Type "WaterResources" in the Name text box.

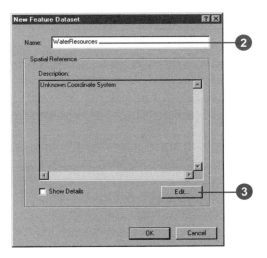

3. Click Edit.

The Spatial Reference Properties dialog box appears. You will import the coordinate system information from one of the coverages.

4. Click Import.

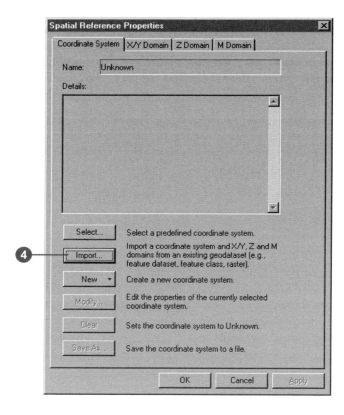

The Browse for Dataset dialog box appears.

5. Navigate to the TopologyData folder in the BuildingaGeodatabase folder. The default installation path is C:\arcgis\ArcTutor\BuildingaGeodatabase.

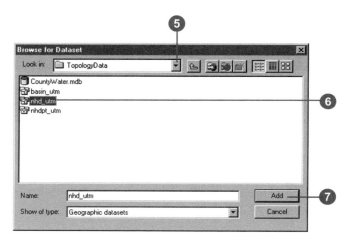

You will import the coordinate system information from the nhd_utm coverage. This coverage is an area clipped from one cataloging unit of the National Hydrography Dataset. It has been projected from geographic coordinates into the Universal Transverse Mercator (UTM) coordinate system. The extent of this coverage is the same as the extent of the feature classes that you plan to load into the dataset.

6. Click nhd_utm.

7. Click Add.

The Spatial Reference Properties dialog box now shows the coordinate system information imported from the coverage.

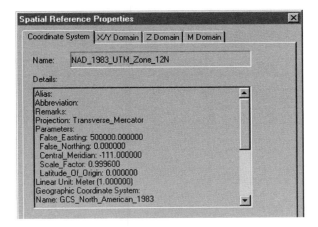

Importing the coordinate system information from an existing coverage or feature class is one way to set the spatial reference for a feature dataset. It is best to use this method when the dataset from which you're importing the coordinate system covers the full extent of all the feature classes that you plan to load into the new dataset.

ArcCatalog sets the precision and XY domain of the dataset using the extent of the data from which you're importing the coordinate system information. This has the advantage of guaranteeing that the source data will fit within the dataset and be stored with the maximum possible precision. However, the maximum precision is not necessarily the best precision, and the default XY domain is typically only about two times the extent of

the coordinate system source dataset's largest dimension. If you expect that you will need to add data beyond this extent, you should manually set the precision and XY domain of the dataset. You cannot load a feature class into a dataset if it has coordinates that fall outside the dataset's XY domain, and you cannot change the XY domain of a dataset after it has been created.

8. Click the X/Y Domain tab.

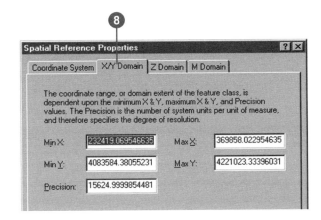

The default minimum and maximum X and Y values are adequate to store this data, but your county is somewhat larger than this small watershed, and you plan to add some data from surrounding counties at a later date. You will need to change the XY domain values.

The default extent of this dataset is about 137 km in the X and Y dimensions. For such a small area, the geodatabase is able to store coordinate values very precisely—in fact, much more precisely than the quality of this data warrants.

The geodatabase stores coordinates in storage units that have integer values. It uses the precision as a scale factor to convert the coordinates to floating point coordinate system unit values for ArcMap. The precision indicates how many storage units are allocated to each coordinate system unit. The coordinate system units for this dataset are meters, and as there are about 2.14 billion internal storage units available to the geodatabase to store the 137,000 m (137 km) extent, the current default precision of 15,624 storage units per meter will store coordinates to less than one-tenth of a millimeter. Increasing the extent of the dataset will decrease the precision because of the fixed number of internal storage units.

Your best data is accurate to a couple of meters, but you plan to add other data to the dataset in the future that is accurate to a couple of centimeters. When you change the extent of the data, you will set the precision to be certain that, in the future, the dataset will be able to store better quality data with adequate precision.

Because you work closely with neighboring counties, you plan to eventually add data that extends 200 km to the west, 200 km to the south, 200 km to the north, and 600 km to the east. The current minimum X value for the dataset is 232,419.069546635 meters. You want to be able to add data up to 200 km to the west, so you

subtract 200,000 meters from the current minimum X to get a new minimum X value of 32,419.069546635. This rounds to 32,419.

9. Type "32419" in the Min X text box.

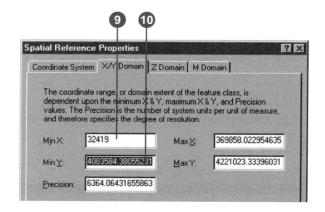

10. Double-click the contents of the Min Y textbox.

You want to be able to store data up to 200 km to the south, so you'll subtract 200,000 from the current Min Y value to get 3,883,584.38055231. This rounds to 3,883,584.

11. Type "3883584" in the MinY text box.

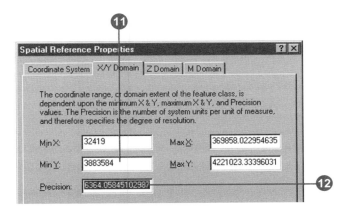

12. Double-click the Precision text box.

The precision was recalculated when you increased the extent of the dataset by decreasing the minimum X and Y values that it can store. The present value, approximately 6364, will allow the dataset to store data with a fraction of a millimeter-level accuracy. As you anticipate needing only centimeter-level accuracy, you'll change the precision to 100. This will allocate 100 internal storage units to each meter—one for each centimeter.

13. Type "100" in the Precision text box.

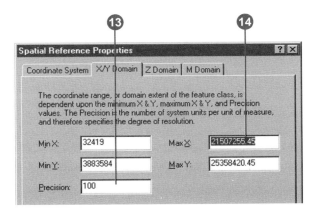

14. Double-click the Max X text box.

The maximum X and Y values were recalculated when you changed the precision and selected the Max X text box. The new maximum X value is 21,507,255.45. The old maximum X value was 369,858. You were planning to increase it to allow data from as far as 600,000 meters (600 km) to the east. As 21,507,255.45 is significantly more than 969,858, there will be enough room to add data to the east.

Similarly, the new Max Y value of 25,358,420.45 is greater than the 4,421,023.0 that you would need to ensure that data as far as 200 km north of the default extent could be added.

15. Click OK.

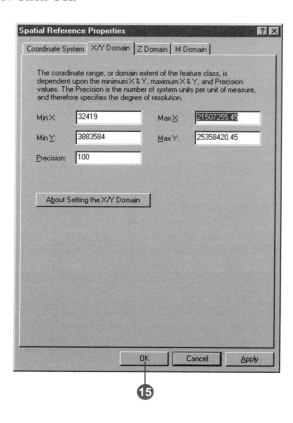

15

You've set the coordinate system and defined the XY domain for the dataset so it can contain data for the area you need at the right precision.

16. Click OK.

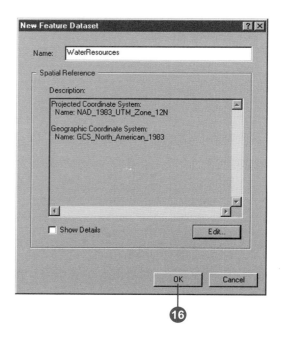

16

The new WaterResources dataset is created in the CountyWater personal geodatabase.

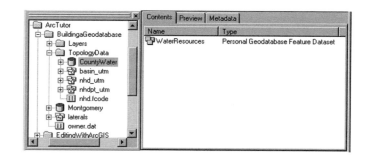

In the next section, you'll explore the coverages that contain the feature classes that you will add to the new dataset.

Exploring coverage feature classes

Coverages may contain a number of feature classes. The data that you will import into the dataset is stored in several feature classes in three different coverages.

1. Click the plus sign to expand the nhd_utm coverage.

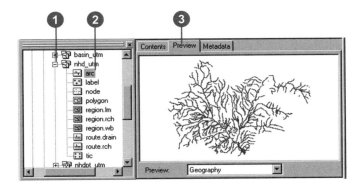

2. Click the arc feature class.
3. Click the Preview tab.

   You can see the features that are stored in this feature class.

   The feature classes in coverages are topologically related to each other. The first feature class listed in this coverage is an arc feature class. Arc feature classes store linear features. In this coverage, there are two route

feature classes. Routes are linear features that are collections of the features in the arc feature class. There is a single polygon feature class. Polygon feature classes are built from features in the arc and label feature classes. Each polygon is defined by a set of linear features from the arc feature class and has attributes stored with a label point from the label feature class. In this coverage, there are three region feature classes. Regions are area features that are collections of features from the polygon feature class.

4. Click the Zoom In tool.

5. Click and drag a box around the southeastern part of the arc feature class in the Preview tab.

You can see a pattern that is like a stream channel system, except that it has some extra lines. These lines are present to define features in the polygon feature class.

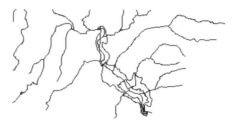

6. Click the polygon feature class.

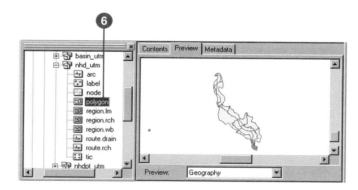

You can see a group of area features that look like puzzle pieces fitted together in the shape of a reservoir.

7. Click region.wb.

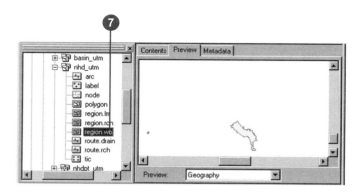

Now you can see a smaller area feature that is not divided into parts. This region feature represents the usual fill level of the reservoir. It is composed of some of the features from the polygon feature class.

8. Click region.lm.

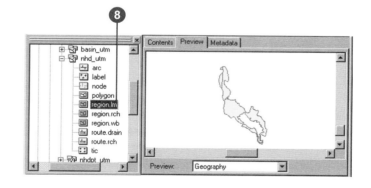

You can see a larger area feature with a hole in it that matches the reservoir. This is the flood zone for the reservoir.

9. Click route.rch.

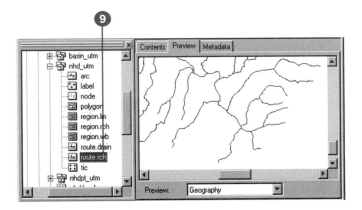

You can see the streams plus flow lines through the reservoir. The lines that define the reservoir and flood zone boundary are not part of this route feature class.

The other two coverages in this folder are basin_utm and nhdpt_utm. The basin_utm coverage has one polygon feature class containing a polygon that defines this watershed, and the nhdpt_utm coverage contains a point feature class with a set of points that shows the locations of springs, wells, and gauging stations within the watershed.

You have explored the contents of the existing coverages. Next, you will load some of the coverage feature classes into your new personal geodatabase dataset.

Loading coverage feature classes into a dataset

You will only load some of the feature classes from these coverages into the new dataset. The arc, label, and polygon feature classes in the nhd_utm coverage do not need to be loaded because they exist only to support the route and region feature classes. Similarly, the arc and label feature classes in basin_utm do not need to be loaded, as they only support the polygon feature class.

1. Navigate to the WaterResources dataset that you created in the CountyWater personal geodatabase.

2. Right-click the WaterResources dataset, point to Import, and click Feature Class (multiple).

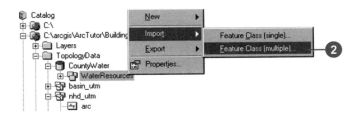

You will load the stream data first.

3. Move the Feature Class to Geodatabase (multiple) dialog box so you can see it and the Catalog tree side by side.

6. Click the plus sign to expand the basin_utm coverage.

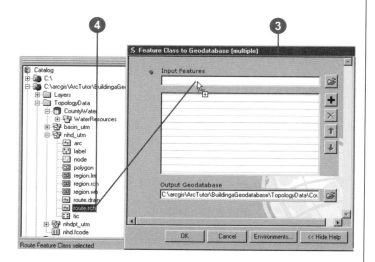

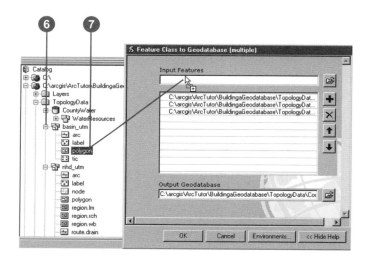

4. Click and drag the route.rch feature class to the Input Features text box of the Feature Class to Geodatabase (multiple) dialog box.

The route.rch feature class is added to the list of feature classes that will be loaded into the geodatabase.

5. Use the same technique to add the region.wb and region.lm feature classes from the nhd_utm coverage to the list.

7. Click and drag the polygon feature class of the basin_utm coverage to the Input Features text box of the Feature Class to Geodatabase (multiple) dialog box.

8. Click the plus sign to expand the nhdpt_utm coverage.

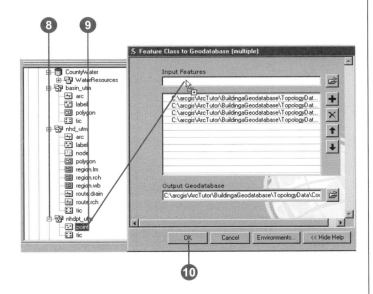

9. Click and drag the point feature class of the nhdpt_utm coverage to the Input Features text box of the Feature Class to Geodatabase (multiple) dialog box.

10. Click OK.

The feature classes are loaded into the feature dataset.

11. Click Done.

If you choose to skip the data loading process, you can find a compressed copy of the final geodatabase, named CountyWater.zip, in the TopologyData folder.

Renaming the feature classes

Now that the feature classes have been loaded, you will give them more descriptive names.

1. Double-click the WaterResources feature dataset.

2. Right-click basin_utm_polygon and click Rename.

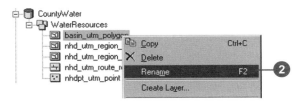

3. Type "watershed" and press the Enter key.

4. Use the same technique to change the names for the other feature classes, using the table below.

Feature class name	New feature class name
basin_utm:	
basin_utm_polygon	watershed
nhd_utm:	
nhd_utm_region_wb	waterbodies
nhd_utm_region_lm	floodzones
nhd_utm_route_rch	streams
nhdpt_utm:	
nhdpt_utm_point	hydro_points

Creating a topology

Now that the feature classes have been renamed, you will create a topology to regulate certain spatial relationships between and within these feature classes.

1. Right-click the WaterResources feature dataset, point to New, and click Topology.

2. Click Next.

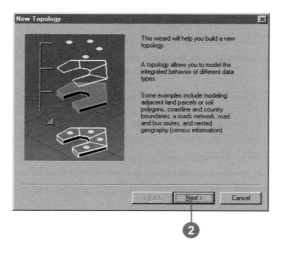

The default cluster tolerance is based on the precision that was set when you specified the XY domain of the dataset. Parts of features within 0.02 meters of each other will be snapped together when the topology is validated.

You could use this dialog box to rename the topology or increase the cluster tolerance. Increasing the cluster tolerance to 0.5, for example, would cause vertices of features within 0.5 meters of each other to be snapped together. For this exercise, you will accept the default name and cluster tolerance.

3. Click Next.

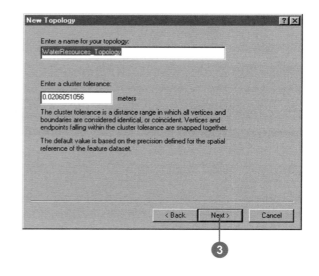

4. Click Select All.

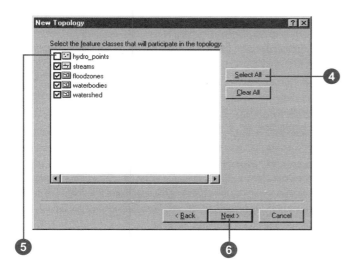

All but one of these feature classes will participate in the topology.

5. Uncheck hydro_points.

You do not need to manage any spatial relationships for these point features.

6. Click Next.

7. Click in the Rank column for the watershed feature class and click 5.

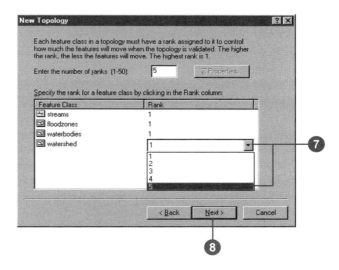

The watershed feature class contains the least accurate data in the dataset. It was heads-up digitized around the streams upstream from the reservoir to create an approximate boundary. Since it is lower quality data, you should set it to a lower rank of 5. This will prevent features in higher ranking feature classes from being snapped to it when the topology is validated. The other feature classes are all of equal accuracy, so you'll leave them at rank 1.

8. Click Next.

There are a number of spatial relationships that you will regulate with this topology. You want to be sure that features in all the feature classes do not overlap, that the area features in the floodzones and waterbodies feature classes do not overlap each other, and that the stream features do not have pseudonodes.

9. Click Add Rule.

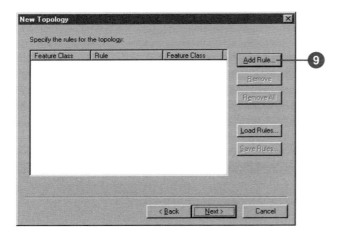

10. Click the Features of feature class dropdown arrow and click streams.

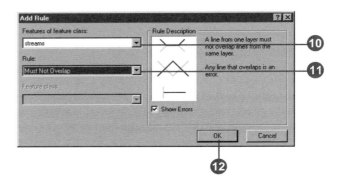

11. Click the Rule dropdown arrow and click Must Not Overlap.

12. Click OK.

The rule is added to the list on this panel of the wizard.

You would ordinarily continue adding topology rules for each of the topological relationships that you want to define. The rules for this topology have been stored in a rule set file, so you will load them.

13. Click Load Rules.

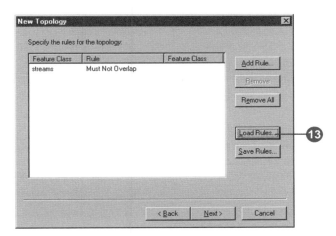

14. Navigate to the TopologyData folder. The default installation path is C:\arcgis\ArcTutor\BuildingaGeodatabase.

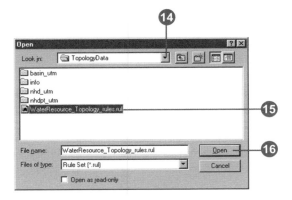

15. Click WaterResource_Topology_rules.rul.

16. Click Open.

The Load Rules dialog box appears. If the feature classes mentioned in the rules do not have the same names as the feature classes in the dataset, you can use this dialog box to match them.

17. Click OK.

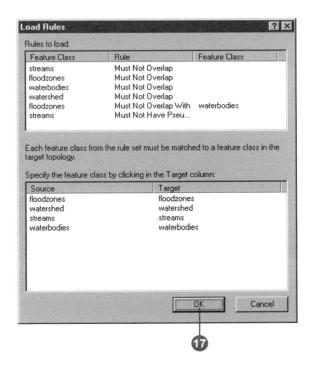

The rules are added to the topology.

18. Click Next.

19. Click Finish.

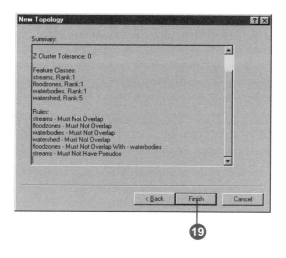

20. Click Yes.

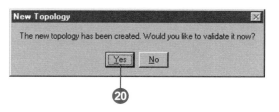

The new topology is added to the dataset and validated.

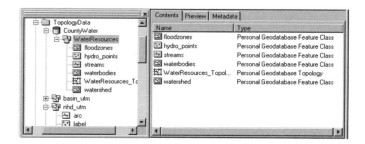

In this exercise, you learned how to create a geodatabase and a new dataset for loading topological data. You defined the coordinate system and spatial reference, allowing room to expand your data and specifying the precision with which it would be stored. You loaded topological data from coverages, leaving out unnecessary feature classes. Finally, you created a geodatabase topology to define a specific set of permissible spatial relationships between features within feature classes and between feature classes.

In the first exercise in this chapter, you learned how to begin organizing data for a geodatabase in ArcCatalog. To learn more about organizing data with ArcCatalog, see the 'Spatial adjustment' chapters in *Building a Geodatabase* and *Using ArcCatalog*.

In Exercise 2, you learned how to import tables and feature classes into a geodatabase. To learn more about importing data, see the 'Migrating existing data into a geodatabase' and 'Topology' chapters in *Building a Geodatabase*.

In Exercise 3, you learned how to create subtypes and attribute domains in a geodatabase. To learn more about subtypes and attribute domains, see the 'Subtypes and attribute domains' chapter in *Building a Geodatabase*.

In Exercise 4, you learned how to create relationships between objects in a geodatabase. To learn more about geodatabase relationship classes, see the 'Defining relationship classes' chapter in *Building a Geodatabase*.

In Exercise 5, you learned how to build a geometric network in a geodatabase. To learn more about geometric networks, see the 'Geometric networks' chapter in *Building a Geodatabase*.

In Exercise 6, you learned how to create feature-linked annotation in a geodatabase. To learn more about geodatabase annotation, see the 'Managing annotation' chapter in *Building a Geodatabase*.

In Exercise 7, you learned how to create layers pointing to feature classes in a geodatabase. To learn more about creating layers to symbolize your data, see *Using ArcMap* and *Using ArcCatalog*.

In Exercise 8, you learned how to create a geodatabase topology. To learn more about creating topology in a geodatabase, see the 'Topology' chapter in *Building a Geodatabase*.

In Exercise 9, you learned how to create a new dataset in which to load topological data and how to create a new topology. To learn more about creating topology in a geodatabase, see the 'Topology' chapter in *Building a Geodatabase*.

Glossary

absolute mode

See digitizing mode.

active data frame

The data frame in a map that is currently being worked on—for example, the data frame to which layers are being added. The active data frame is shown in bold text in the ArcMap table of contents.

alias

An alternative name specified for fields, tables, and feature classes that is more descriptive and user-friendly than the actual name of these items. In database management systems, aliases can contain characters, such as spaces, that can't be included in the actual names.

aligned dimension

A dimension that runs parallel to the baseline and represents the true distance between the beginning and end dimension points. ArcGIS supports aligned and linear dimension features.

annotation

Descriptive text used to label features on or around a map. Information stored for annotation includes a text string, a position at which it can be displayed, and display characteristics.

ArcInfo workspace

A file-based collection of coverages, grids, TINs, or shapefiles stored as a directory of folders in the file system.

arc–node topology

The data structure in a coverage used to represent linear features and polygon boundaries, and to support analysis functions, such as network tracing. Nodes represent the beginning and ending vertices of each arc. Arcs that share a node are connected, and polygons are defined by a series of connected arcs. An arc that intersects another arc is split into two arcs. Each arc that defines all or part of a polygon boundary records the number of the polygon to its left and to its right, giving it a direction of travel.

ArcSDE

Server software that provides ArcSDE® clients (e.g., ArcGIS Desktop, ArcGIS Server, ArcIMS) a gateway for storing, managing, and using spatial data in one of the following commercial database management systems: IBM® DB2® UDB, IBM Informix®, Microsoft® SQL Server™, and Oracle®.

attribute

Information about a geographic feature in a GIS, generally stored in a table with the feature or linked to the feature by a unique identifier. Attributes of a river might include its name, length, and average depth.

attribute domain

In a geodatabase, a mechanism for enforcing data integrity. Attribute domains define what values are allowed in a field in a feature class or nonspatial attribute table. If the features or nonspatial objects have been grouped into subtypes, different attribute domains can be assigned to each of the subtypes. Types of attribute domains include range and coded value domains.

attribute table

A database or tabular file containing information about a set of geographic features, usually arranged so that each row represents a feature and each column represents one feature attribute. In raster datasets, each row of an attribute table corresponds to a certain region of cells having the same value. In a GIS, attribute tables are often joined or related to spatial data layers, and the attribute values they contain can be used to find, query, and symbolize features or raster cells.

Attributes dialog box

In ArcMap, a dialog box that displays attributes of selected features for editing.

behavior

Properties of an object in a geodatabase that describe how it can be edited and drawn. Behavior includes, but is not limited to, validation rules, subtypes, default values, and relationships.

buffer

A zone of a specified distance around features. Buffers are useful for proximity analysis—for example, to find all stream segments within 300 feet of a proposed logging area.

CAD

A computer-based system for the design, drafting, and display of graphical information. Also known as computer-aided drafting, such systems are most commonly used to support engineering, planning, and illustrating activities.

CAD feature class

A read-only member of a CAD feature dataset, comprised of one of the following: polylines, points, polygons, multi-patch, or annotation. The feature attribute table of a CAD feature class is a virtual table composed of select CAD graphic properties and any existing field attribute values.

centroid

The geometric center of a feature. Of a line, it is the midpoint; of a polygon, the center of area; of a three-dimensional figure, the center of volume.

check in

The procedure that transfers a copy of data into a master geodatabase, overwriting the original copy of that data and reenabling it so it can be accessed and saved from that location.

check out

A procedure that records the duplication of data from one geodatabase to another and disables the original data so that both versions cannot be accessed or saved at the same time.

check-out geodatabase

A personal or ArcSDE geodatabase that contains data checked out from a master geodatabase.

check-out version

The data version created in a check-out geodatabase when data is checked out to that database. This version is created as a copy of the synchronization version. Only the edits made to this check-out version can be checked back into the master geodatabase.

See also check-out geodatabase, master check-out version.

circle

A geometric shape for which the distance from the center to any point on the edge is equal; the closed plane curve defining such a shape or the surface bounded by such a curve.

circular arc

A line with two vertices, one situated at each endpoint, rather than a line composed of numerous vertices with line segments between them. ArcMap offers several ways to create circular arcs. These include the Arc tool, the Endpoint Arc tool, the Tangent Curve tool, and the Tangent Curve command.

cluster tolerance

The minimum distance between vertices in the topology. Vertices that fall within the cluster tolerance will be snapped together during the validate topology process. The default cluster tolerance is the minimum possible cluster tolerance, based on the precision and extent defined for the spatial reference of the dataset. See also fuzzy tolerance, used analogously in coverage data model.

clustering

A part of the topology validation process in which vertices that fall within the cluster tolerance are snapped together.

coincident

Occupying the same space. Coincident features or parts of features occupy the same space in the same plane. In geodatabase feature classes, vertices or boundaries that fall within the set cluster tolerance of one another are coincident; they are snapped together during the validate topology process.

column

The vertical dimension of a table. Each column stores the values of one type of attribute for all of the records, or rows, in the table. All the values in a given column are of the same data type—for example, number, string, BLOB, date.

compression

A reduction of file size for data handling or storage. For ArcSDE geodatabases, the compress command improves database performance by removing redundant rows shared by multiple versions. The process can only be run by the ArcSDE administrator. Personal geodatabases should be compressed periodically to reduce their size, especially after editing.

computer-aided design

See CAD.

conflict

Conflicts occur when the same feature or topologically related features are edited in both the edit and reconciliation versions, and it is unclear in the database which representation is valid. Resolving the conflict requires you to make the decision as to the feature's correct representation using the Conflict Resolution dialog box.

connectivity

1. The way in which features in a GIS database are attached to one another functionally or spatially.

2. In a geodatabase, the state of edges and junctions in a logical network that controls flow, tracing, and pathfinding.

3. The topological identification in a coverage of connected arcs by recording the from- and to-node for each arc. Arcs that share a common node are connected. See also arc–node topology.

connectivity rules

A rule that constrains the type and number of network features that can be connected to one another in a geodatabase. There are two types of connectivity rules: edge–junction and edge–edge.

constraints

Limits imposed on a model to maintain data integrity. For example, in a water network model, an 8-inch pipe cannot connect to a 4-inch pipe.

construct features

The process of taking selected features from one or more feature classes and creating new features in a target feature class in an edit session. The Construct Features tool uses the input geometries of the selected features to construct polygons or lines following polygon boundaries, depending on the geometry of the target feature class.

contiguity

1. The state of lying next to or close to one another.

2. In a coverage, the topological identification of adjacent polygons by recording the left and right polygon for each arc.

control

In mapping, a system of points with established horizontal and vertical positions that are used as fixed references for known ground points or specific locations. The establishment of controls is one of the first steps involved in digitizing.

control points

See control.

coordinate

A set of numbers that designate location in a given reference system such as x,y in a planar coordinate system or x,y,z in a three-dimensional coordinate system. Coordinates represent locations on the earth's surface relative to other locations.

coordinate system

1. A reference system used to measure horizontal and vertical distances on a planimetric map. A coordinate system is usually defined by a map projection; a spheroid of reference; a datum; one or more standard parallels; a central meridian; and possible shifts in the x- and y-directions to locate x,y positions of point, line, and area features.

2. In ArcInfo, a system with units and characteristics defined by a map projection. A common coordinate system is used to spatially register geographic data for the same area.

coverage

A file-based vector data storage format for storing the location, shape, and attributes of geographic features. A coverage usually represents a single theme, such as soils, streams, roads, or land use. It is one of the primary vector data storage formats for ArcInfo.

A coverage stores geographic features as primary features, such as arcs, nodes, polygons, and label points, and secondary features, such as tics, map extent, links, and annotation.

Associated feature attribute tables describe and store attributes of the geographic features.

cracking

A part of the topology validation process in which vertices are created at the intersection of feature edges.

current task

During editing in ArcMap, a setting in the Current Task dropdown list that determines with which task the sketch construction tools—Sketch, Arc, Distance–Distance, and Intersection—will work. The current task is set by clicking a task in the Current Task dropdown list. All tasks in the Current Task dropdown list work with a sketch that you create—for example, the Create New Feature task uses a sketch you create to make a new feature. The Extend/Trim Feature task uses a sketch you create to determine where the selected feature will be extended or trimmed. The Cut Polygon Feature task uses a sketch you create to determine where the polygon will be cut.

custom behavior

Behavior is the implementation of an object class method. ESRI-provided objects have a set of methods associated with them. A developer can choose to override one of these methods or create additional methods. In this instance, the object is said to have custom behavior.

custom feature

A feature with specialized behavior instantiated in a class by a developer.

custom object

Objects that have custom behavior provided by a developer.

dangle tolerance

The minimum length allowed for dangling arcs in coverages in the ArcInfo Clean process. Clean removes dangling arcs that are shorter than the dangle length. Also known as the dangle length.

dangling arc

In coverages, an arc having the same polygon on both its left and right sides and having at least one node that does not connect to any other arc. It often identifies where a polygon does not close properly—for example, undershoot—where arcs don't connect properly, or where an arc was digitized past its intersection with another arc—for example, overshoot. A dangling arc is not always an error—for example, dangling arcs can represent cul-de-sacs in street centerline maps.

data

A collection of related facts usually arranged in a particular format and gathered for a particular purpose.

data frame

In ArcMap, a frame on the map that displays layers occupying the same geographic area. You may have one or more data frames on your map depending on how you want to organize your data. For instance, one data frame might highlight a study area, and another might provide an overview of where the study area is located.

data integrity

Maintenance of data values according to data model and data type—for example, to maintain integrity, numeric columns will not accept character data.

data source

Any geographic data, such as a coverage, shapefile, raster, or feature class, in a geodatabase.

data type

The characteristic of columns and variables that defines what types of data values they can store. Examples include character, floating point, and integer.

data view

An all-purpose view in ArcMap for exploring, displaying, and querying geographic data. This view hides all map elements such as titles, North arrows, and scalebars. See also layout view.

database

A collection of related files organized for efficient retrieval of information. In the context of an ArcSDE geodatabase, some relational databases group data together in discretely named databases—for example, SQL Server, Sybase®—while others do not—for example, Oracle.

dataset

1. Any feature class, table, or collection of feature classes or tables in the geodatabase.

2. A named collection of logically related data items arranged in a prescribed manner.

dataset precision

The mathematical exactness or detail with which a value is stored within the dataset, based on the number of significant digits that can be stored for each coordinate. In a geodatabase, the precision of the dataset is the number of internal storage units that are allocated to each of the linear units of a coordinate system.

decimal degrees

Degrees of latitude and longitude expressed as a decimal rather than in degrees, minutes, and seconds.

default junction type

Two edge types may be connectable through more than one junction type. You can establish which of those junction types is the default for connecting the two edge types. This junction type is the default junction type.

digitizing

1. To encode geographic features in digital form as x,y coordinates.

2. The process of converting the features on a paper map into digital format. When you digitize a map, you use a digitizing tablet, or digitizer, connected to your computer and trace over features with a digitizer puck, which is similar to a mouse. The x,y coordinates of these features are automatically recorded and stored as spatial data.

digitizing mode

Also called absolute mode, digitizing mode is one of the ways in which a digitizing tablet operates. In digitizing mode, the location of the tablet is mapped to a specific location on the screen. Moving the digitizer puck on the tablet surface causes the screen pointer to move to precisely the same position.

dimension construction methods

Dimension construction methods dictate what type of dimension feature is created and the number of points required to complete the feature's geometry. Construction methods include simple aligned, aligned, linear, rotated linear, free aligned, and free linear.

dimension feature

Dimension features are a special kind of map annotation that show specific lengths or distances on a map. A dimension feature may indicate the length of a side of a building or land parcel, or it may indicate the distance between two features such as a fire hydrant and the corner of a building. Dimension features are stored in a dimension feature class.

dimension feature class

In the geodatabase, dimension features are stored in dimension feature classes. Like other feature classes in the geodatabase, all features in a dimension feature class have a geographic location and attributes and can either be inside or outside a feature dataset.

dimension style

A dimension feature's style describes its symbology, what parts of it are drawn, and how it is drawn. Every time you create a new dimension feature, it is assigned a particular style. A collection of dimension styles is associated with a dimension feature class.

Dimensioning toolbar

A toolbar in ArcMap that facilitates the creation of dimension features.

direct connect

A two-tiered architecture for connecting to spatial databases. Direct connect does not require the ArcSDE application server to connect to a spatial database.

dirty areas

Areas that have been edited after the initial topology validation process. Dirty areas represent regions surrounding features that have been altered and that require an additional topology validation to be performed to discover any topology errors that may be present.

disconnected editing

The process of copying data to another geodatabase, editing that data, then merging the changes with the data in the source or master geodatabase.

distance units

The units—for example, feet, miles, meters, or kilometers—ArcMap uses to report measurements, dimensions of shapes, distance tolerances, and offsets.

double precision

Refers to a high level of coordinate accuracy based on the possible number of significant digits that can be stored for each coordinate. ArcInfo datasets can be stored in either single- or double-precision coordinates. Double-precision coverages store up to 15 significant digits per coordinate—typically, 13 to 14 significant digits—retaining the accuracy of much less than one meter at a global extent. See also single precision.

edge element

See logical network.

edge (topology)

A line segment in a topology that defines lines or polygon boundaries. Multiple features in one or more feature classes may share topology edges.

edge–edge rule

A connectivity rule that establishes that an edge of type A may connect to an edge of type B through a junction of type C. Edge–Edge rules always involve a junction type.

edge–junction cardinality

A rule may exist that allows an edge of type A to connect to a junction of type B. By default, any number of edges of type A can connect to a single junction of type B. You may want to restrict this. You can specify that between two and five edges of type A can connect to a junction of type B; if there are less than two edges, or more than five edges, the connectivity rule is being violated. Similarly, you can restrict the number of junctions of type C that can connect to any junction of type D. This range of permissible connections is edge–junction cardinality.

edge–junction rule

A connectivity rule that establishes that an edge of type A may connect to a junction of type B.

edit cache

See map cache.

edit session

In ArcMap, editing takes place within an edit session. An edit session begins when you click Start Editing on the Editor menu and ends when you click Stop Editing.

Editor toolbar

A toolbar that lets you create and modify features and their attributes in ArcMap.

ellipse

A geometric shape equivalent to a circle that is viewed obliquely; a flattened circle.

error

Violations of a topology rule detected during the topology validation process.

extent

The coordinates defining the minimum bounding rectangle—that is, xmin, ymin and xmax, ymax—of a data source. All coordinates for the data source fall within this boundary.

feature

1. An object class in a geodatabase that has a field of type geometry. Features are stored in feature classes.

2. A representation of a real-world object.

3. A point, line, or polygon in a coverage or shapefile.

feature attribute table

A table used to store attribute information for a specific coverage feature class. ArcInfo maintains the first several items of these tables. Feature attribute tables supported for coverages include the following:

<cover>.PAT	for polygons or points
<cover>.AAT	for arcs
<cover>.NAT	for nodes
<cover>.RAT	for routes
<cover>.SEC	for sections
<cover>.PAT	for regions
<cover>.TAT	for annotation (text)

where <cover> is the coverage name.

feature class

1. The conceptual representation of a category of geographic features. When referring to geographic features, feature classes include point, line, area, and annotation. In a geodatabase, an object class that stores features and has a geometry field type.

2. A classification describing the format of geographic features and supporting data in a coverage. Coverage feature classes for representing geographic features include point, arc, node, route system, route, section, polygon, and region. One or more coverage features are used to model geographic features—for example, arcs and nodes can be used to model linear features such as street centerlines. The tic, annotation, link, and boundary

feature classes provide supporting data for coverage data management and viewing.

3. The collection of all the point, line, or polygon features or annotation in a CAD dataset.

4. In a geodatabase, an object class that stores features and has a field of type geometry.

feature dataset

In geodatabases, a collection of feature classes that share the same spatial reference. Because the feature classes share the same spatial reference, they can participate in topological relationships with each other such as in a geometric network, linear network, or topology. Several feature classes with the same geometry may be stored in the same feature dataset. Object classes and relationship classes can also be stored in a feature dataset.

field

A column in a table. Each field contains the values for a single attribute.

fuzzy tolerance

An extremely small distance used to resolve inexact intersection locations due to the limited arithmetic precision of computers. It defines the resolution of a coverage resulting from the Clean operation or a topological overlay operation such as Union, Intersect, or Clip.

In geodatabase feature classes, this concept is replaced by cluster tolerance.

geodatabase

A geographic database that is hosted inside a relational database management system that provides services for managing geographic data. These services include validation rules, relationships, and topological associations.

geodatabase data model

A geographic data model that represents geographic features as objects in an object relational database. Features are stored as rows in a table; geometry is stored in a shape field. Supports sophisticated modeling of real-world features. Objects may have custom behavior. Compare to the georelational data model.

geometric network

A geometric network can be thought of as a one-dimensional nonplanar graph, or logical network, that is composed of features. These features are constrained to exist within the network and can, therefore, be considered network features. ArcInfo will automatically maintain the explicit topological relationships between network features in a geometric network.

georelational data model

A geographic data model that represents geographic features as an interrelated set of spatial and descriptive data. The georelational model is the fundamental data model used in coverages. Compare to the geodatabase data model.

index

A data structure used in a database to improve query performance. Feature classes also have spatial indexes that improve spatial query performance.

instance

The name of the process running on the ArcSDE server that allows connections and access to spatial data.

intersect

The topological integration of two spatial datasets that preserves features that fall within the area common to both input datasets. See also union.

item

1. A column of information in an INFO table.

2. An element in the Catalog tree. The Catalog tree can contain both geographic data sources and nongeographic elements, such as folders, folder connections, and file types.

junction element

See logical network.

label point

A feature class in a coverage used to represent point features and identify polygons.

layer

1. A collection of similar geographic features, such as rivers, lakes, counties, or cities, of a particular area or place for display on a map. A layer references geographic data stored in a data source, such as a coverage, and defines how to display it. You can create and manage layers as you would any other type of data in your database.

2. A feature class in a shared geodatabase managed with SDE 3.

layout view

The view for laying out your map in ArcMap. Layout view shows the virtual page on which you place and arrange geographic data and map elements, such as titles, legends, and scalebars, for printing. See also data view.

left–right topology

A topological data structure used to represent contiguity between polygons in the coverage data model. Left–right topology supports analysis functions, such as adjacency. See also topology.

linear dimension

A dimension whose length doesn't represent the true distance between the beginning and end dimension points. Linear dimensions can be vertical, horizontal, or rotated. A vertical dimension's line represents the vertical distance between the beginning and end dimension points. A horizontal linear dimension's line represents the horizontal distance between the beginning and end dimension points. A rotated linear dimension is a dimension whose line is at some angle to the baseline and whose length represents the length of the dimension line itself, not the baseline.

logical network

An abstract representation of a network. A logical network consists of edge, junction, and turn elements and the connectivity between them. It does not contain information about the geometry or location of its elements.

map

1. A graphic depiction on a flat surface of the physical features of the whole or a part of the earth or other body, or of the heavens, using shapes to represent objects, and symbols to describe their nature; at a scale whose representative fraction is less than 1:1. Maps generally use a specified projection and indicate the direction of orientation.

2. Any graphical representation of geographic or spatial information.

3. The document used in ArcMap to display and work with geographic data. In ArcMap, a map contains one or more layers of geographic data, contained in data frames, and various supporting map elements, such as a scalebar.

map cache

A setting used in ArcMap that allows temporary storage of geodatabase features from a given map extent in the desktop computer's RAM, which may result in performance improvements in ArcMap for editing, feature rendering, and labeling.

map document

In ArcMap, the disk-based representation of a map. Map documents can be printed or embedded into other documents. Map documents have a .mxd file extension.

map topology

A temporary set of topological relationships between coincident parts of simple features on a map, used to edit shared parts of multiple features.

map units

The units—for example, feet, miles, meters, or kilometers—in which the coordinates of spatial data are stored.

master check-out version

A version in the master geodatabase, created when data is checked out, that represents the state of the data at the time it was checked out.

master geodatabase

An ArcSDE geodatabase from which data has been checked out.

merge policy

In geodatabases, all attribute domains have a merge policy associated with them. When two features are merged into a single feature in ArcMap, the merge policies dictate what happens to the value of the attribute to which the domain is associated. Standard merge policies are default value, sum, and weighted average.

minimum bounding rectangle

A rectangle, oriented to the x- and y-axes, that bounds a geographic feature or a geographic dataset. It is specified by two coordinates: xmin, ymin and xmax, ymax—for example, the extent defines a minimum bounding rectangle for a coverage.

multipart feature

A feature that is composed of more than one physical part but only references one set of attributes in the database—for example, in a layer of states, the state of Hawaii could be considered a multipart feature. Although composed of many islands, it would be recorded in the database as one feature.

multipoint feature

A feature that consists of more than one point but only references one set of attributes in the database—for example, a system of oil wells might be considered a multipoint feature, as there is a single set of attributes for the main well and multiple well holes.

multiuser geodatabase

A geodatabase in an RDBMS served to client applications—for example, ArcMap—by ArcSDE. Multiuser geodatabases can be very large and support multiple concurrent editors. They are supported on a variety of commercial RDBMSs, including Oracle, Microsoft SQL Server, IBM DB2, and Informix.

network trace

A function that follows connectivity in a geometric network. Specific kinds of network tracing include finding features that are connected, finding common ancestors, finding loops, tracing upstream, and tracing downstream.

See also geometric network.

node

An endpoint of a topology edge. Topology nodes may also be introduced along an edge during editing.

null value

The absence of a value. A geographic feature for which there is no associated attribute information.

object

The representation of a real-world entity stored in a geodatabase. An object has properties and behavior.

object class

A collection of objects in the geodatabase that have the same behavior and the same set of attributes. All objects in the geodatabase are stored in object classes.

overshoot

That portion of an arc digitized past its intersection with another arc. See also dangling arc.

pan

To move the viewing window up, down, or sideways to display areas in a geographic dataset that, at the current viewing scale, lie outside the viewing window.

password

A secret series of characters that enables a user to access a computer, data file, or program. The user must enter his or her password before the computer will respond to commands. The password helps ensure that unauthorized users do not access the computer, file, or program.

personal geodatabase

A geodatabase, usually on the same network as the client application—for example, ArcMap—that supports one editor at a time. Personal geodatabases are managed in a Microsoft Jet Engine database. Personal geodatabases can contain geometric networks, linear networks, and topologies and can be used as check-out databases for disconnected editing of geographic data in the field.

planarize

The process of creating multiple line features by splitting longer features at the places where they intersect other line features. This process can be useful when you have nontopological line work that has been spaghetti digitized or imported from a computer-aided design (CAD) drawing.

point

A single x,y coordinate that represents a single geographic feature such as a telephone pole.

point mode digitizing

One of two methods of digitizing features using the ArcMap Editor's Sketch tool or from a paper map using a digitizer. With point mode digitizing, you can create or edit features by digitizing a series of precise points, or vertices. Point mode digitizing is effective when precise digitizing is required—for example, when digitizing a perfectly straight line. See also stream mode digitizing.

polygon

A two-dimensional feature representing an area such as a state or county.

post

During versioned geodatabase editing, the process of applying the current edit session to the reconciled target version.

preliminary topology

In coverages, refers to incomplete region or polygon topology. Region topology defines region–arc and region–polygon relationships. A topological region has both the region–arc and the region–polygon relationships. A preliminary region has the region–arc relationship but not the region–polygon relationship. In other words, preliminary regions have no polygon topology. Polygon topology defines polygon–arc–label point relationships. A preliminary polygon has the polygon–label point relationship but not the polygon–arc relationship. Coverages with preliminary topology have red in their icons in the Catalog.

projection

A mathematical formula that transforms feature locations from the earth's curved surface to a map's flat surface. A projected coordinate system employs a projection to transform locations expressed as latitude and longitude values to x,y coordinates. Projections cause distortions in one or more of these spatial properties: distance, area, shape, and direction.

property

An attribute of an object defining one of its characteristics or an aspect of its behavior. For example, the Visible property affects whether a control can be seen at runtime. You can set an item's properties using its Properties dialog box.

pseudonode

A node connecting only two edges or a logical split defined in the topology cache while editing. Pseudonodes of the latter sort become a vertex after editing.

pull check-in

A check-in operation initiated from a master geodatabase.

push check-in

A check-in operation initiated from a check-out geodatabase.

pyramids

In raster datasets, reduced resolution layers, or pyramids, record the original data in decreasing levels of resolution. The coarsest level of resolution is used to quickly draw the entire dataset. As you zoom in, layers with finer resolutions are drawn; performance is maintained because you're drawing successively smaller areas.

query

A question or request used for selecting features. A query often appears in the form of a statement or logical expression. In ArcMap, a query contains a field, an operator, and a value.

radius

The distance from the center to the outer edge of a circle or circular curve.

rank

A method of assigning an accuracy value to feature classes to avoid having vertices from a feature class collected with a high level of accuracy being snapped to vertices from a less accurate feature class. Vertices from higher ranking feature classes will not be moved when snapping with vertices with lower ranked feature classes. The highest rank is 1, and you can assign up to 50 different ranks.

raster

Represents any data source that uses a grid structure to store geographic information.

RDBMS

Relational database management system. A database management system with the ability to access data organized in tabular files that can be related to each other by a common field (item). An RDBMS has the capability to recombine the data items from different files, providing powerful tools for data usage. ArcSDE supports several commercial RDBMSs.

reconcile

Reconciling is the process of merging all modified datasets, feature classes, and tables in the current edit session and a second target version. All features and rows that do not conflict are merged into the edit session, replacing the current features or rows. Features that are modified in each version are conflicts and require further resolution via the Conflict Resolution dialog box.

record

1. In an attribute table, a single row of thematic descriptors. In SQL terms, a record is analogous to a tuple.

2. A logical unit of data in a file—for example, there is one record in the ARC file for each arc in a coverage.

reference data

Tables or feature classes containing address information that geocoding services use to find the locations of addresses.

relate

An operation that establishes a temporary connection between corresponding records in two tables using an item common to both—for example, key attributes. Each record in one table is connected to those records in the other table that share the same value for the common item. See also relational join.

relational join

The operation of relating and physically merging two attribute tables using their common item.

relationship

An association or link between two or more objects in a geodatabase. Relationships can exist between spatial objects (features in feature classes) or nonspatial objects (rows in a table), or between spatial and nonspatial objects.

relationship class

Objects in a real-world system often have particular associations with other objects in the database. These kinds of associations between objects in the geodatabase are called relationships. Relationships can exist between spatial objects (features in feature classes), nonspatial objects (rows in a table), or between spatial and nonspatial objects. While spatial objects are stored in the geodatabase in feature classes, and nonspatial objects are stored in object classes, relationships are stored in relationship classes.

row

1. A record in an attribute table. The horizontal dimension of a table composed of a set of columns containing one data item each.

2. A horizontal group of cells in a raster.

rule (connectivity)

A constraint on the type of network features that may be connected to one another and the number of features of any particular type that can be connected to features of another type. There are two types of connectivity rules: edge–junction and edge–edge rules.

rule (topology)

An instruction to the geodatabase defining the permissible relationships of features within a given feature class or between features in two different feature classes. Topology rules are compared against the features in the feature class during the topology validation process and violations are marked as errors. After the topology validation process, the errors can be corrected by editing the feature class; occasionally, violations of a topology rule may represent acceptable conditions. In these cases, the errors can be marked as exceptions.

scanning

The process of capturing data in raster format with a device called a scanner. Some scanners also use software to convert raster data to vector data.

schema

The structure or design of a database.

schema-only check-out

A type of check-out that creates the schema of the data being checked out in the check-out geodatabase but does not copy any data.

segment

A line that connects vertices—for example, in a sketch of a building, a segment would represent one wall.

select

To choose from a number or group of features or records; to create a separate set or subset.

Selectable layers

Layers from which features can be selected in ArcMap with the interactive selection tools. Selectable layers can be chosen using the Set Selectable Layers command in the Selection menu, or on the optional Selection tab in the table of contents.

selected set

A subset of the features in a layer or records in a table. ArcMap provides several ways to select features and records graphically or according to their attribute values.

selection anchor

When editing in ArcMap, a small x located in the center of selected features. The selection anchor is used when you move features using snapping. It is the point on the feature or group of features that will be snapped to the snapping location. This is also the point around which your selection will rotate when you use the Rotate tool and around which your feature will scale when you use the Scale tool. You can reposition the selection anchor.

server

The computer where the ArcSDE geodatabase you want to access is located.

shape

The characteristic appearance or visible form of a geographic object. Geographic objects can be represented on a map using one of three basic shapes: points, lines, or polygons.

shapefile

A vector data storage format for storing the location, shape, and attributes of geographic features. A shapefile is stored in a set of related files and contains one feature class.

shared boundary

A segment or boundary common to two features—for example, in a parcel database, adjacent parcels will share a boundary. Another example might be a parcel that shares a boundary on one side with a river. The segment of the river that coincides with the parcel boundary would share the same coordinates as the parcel boundary.

shared vertex

A vertex common to multiple features—for example, in a parcel database, adjacent parcels will share a vertex at the common corner.

simple feature

A point, line, or polygon that is not part of a geometric network and is not an annotation feature, dimension feature, or custom object.

single precision

Refers to a level of coordinate accuracy based on the number of significant digits that can be stored for each coordinate. Single-precision numbers store up to seven significant digits for each coordinate, retaining a precision of ±5 meters in an extent of 1,000,000 meters. ArcInfo datasets can be stored as either single- or double-precision coordinates. See also double precision.

sketch

When editing in ArcMap, a shape that represents a feature's geometry. Every existing feature on a map has an alternate form, a sketch. A sketch lets you see exactly how a feature is composed, with all vertices and segments of the feature visible. To modify a feature, you must modify its sketch. To create a feature, you must first create a sketch. You can only create line and polygon sketches, as points have neither vertices nor segments.

Sketches help complete the current task—for example, the Create New Feature task uses a sketch you create to make a new feature. The Extend/Trim Feature task uses a sketch you create to determine where the selected feature will be extended or trimmed. The Cut Polygon Feature task uses a sketch you create to determine where the polygon will be cut into two features.

sketch constraints

In ArcMap editing, an angle or length limitation that can be placed on segments created using the Sketch tool.

sketch operations

In ArcMap, editing operations that are performed on an existing sketch. Examples are Insert Vertex, Delete Vertex, Flip, Trim, Delete Sketch, Finish Sketch, and Finish Part. All of these operations are available from the Sketch context menu, which is available when you right-click any part of a sketch using any editing tool.

snapping

The process of moving a feature to coincide exactly with coordinates of another feature within a specified snapping distance or tolerance.

snapping environment

Settings in ArcMap Editor's Snapping Environment window and Editing Options dialog box that help you establish exact locations in relation to other features. You determine the snapping environment by setting a snapping tolerance, snapping properties, and a snapping priority.

snapping priority

During ArcMap editing, the order in which snapping will occur by layer. You can set the snapping priority by dragging the layer names in the Snapping Environment window to new locations.

snapping properties

In ArcMap editing, a combination of a shape to snap to and a method for what part of the shape you will snap to. You can set your snapping properties to have a feature snap to a vertex, edge, or endpoint of features in a specific layer—for example, a layer snapping property might let you snap to the vertices of buildings. A more generic, sketch-specific snapping property might let you snap to the vertices of a sketch you're creating.

snapping tolerance

The distance within which the pointer or a feature will snap to another location during ArcMap editing.

If the location being snapped to (vertex, boundary, midpoint, or connection) is within the distance you set, the pointer will automatically snap. For example, if you want to snap a power line to a utility pole and the snapping tolerance is set to 25 pixels, whenever the power line comes within a 25-pixel range of the pole, it will automatically snap to it. Snapping tolerance can be measured using either map units or pixels.

spatial database

Any DBMS that contains spatial data.

spatial domain

Describes the range and precision of x,y coordinates and z- and m-values that can be stored in a feature dataset or feature class in a geodatabase.

spatial join

A type of spatial analysis in which the attributes of features in two different layers are joined together based on the relative locations of the features.

spatial reference

Describes both the projection and spatial domain extent for a feature dataset or feature class in a geodatabase.

split policy

All attribute domains have a split policy associated with them. When a feature is split into two new features in the ArcMap Editor, the split policies dictate what happens to the value of the attribute to which the domain is associated. Standard split policies are duplicate, default value, and geometry ratio.

SQL

Structured Query Language. A syntax for defining and manipulating data from a relational database. Developed by IBM in the 1970s, it has become an industry standard for query languages in most relational database management systems.

stream mode digitizing

One of two methods of digitizing features from a paper map. Also known as streaming, stream mode digitizing provides an easy way to capture features when you don't require much precision—for example, to digitize rivers, streams, and contour lines. With stream mode, you create the first vertex of the feature and trace over the rest of the feature with the digitizer puck. You can also use digitize in stream mode with the ArcMap Sketch tool when editing freehand. See also point mode digitizing.

stream tolerance

The minimum distance the pointer must be moved from the last vertex before the next vertex will be created when using the Sketch tool in stream mode.

When streaming, vertices are automatically created at a defined interval as you move the mouse—for example, if the stream tolerance is set to 10 map units, you must move the pointer at least 10 map units before the next vertex will be created. If you move the pointer more than 10 map units, there may be more space between vertices, but there will always be a minimum interval of 10 map units. Stream tolerance is measured in map units.

subtypes

Although all objects in a feature class or object class must have the same behavior and attributes, not all objects have to share the same default values and validation rules. You can group features and objects into subtypes. Subtypes differentiate objects based on their rules.

symbol

A graphic pattern used to represent a feature—for example, line symbols represent arc features; marker symbols, points; shade symbols, polygons; and text symbols, annotation. Many characteristics define symbols, including color, size, angle, and pattern.

symbology

The criteria used to determine symbols for the features in a layer. A characteristic of a feature may influence the size, color, and shape of the symbol used.

synchronization version

A version created in a check-out ArcSDE geodatabase when a check-out is made to that geodatabase. This version is created as a child of the DEFAULT version and represents the state of the data at the time the check-out was created.

table

Information formatted in rows and columns. A set of data elements that has a horizontal dimension (rows) and a vertical dimension (columns) in an RDBMS. A table has a specified number of columns but can have any number of rows. See also attribute table.

table of contents

In ArcMap, lists all the data frames and layers on the map and shows what the features in each layer represent.

tabular data

Descriptive information that is stored in rows and columns and can be linked to map features.

tagged values

Tagged values are used to set additional properties of UML elements—for example, you can set the length, in characters, of a string field using a tagged value.

target layer

Used in ArcMap editing, a setting in the Target layer dropdown list that determines to which layer new features will be added. The target layer is set by clicking a layer in the Target layer dropdown list. For instance, if you set the target layer to Buildings, any features you create will be part of the Buildings layer. You must set the target layer whenever you're creating new features—whether you're creating them with the Sketch tool, by copying and pasting, or by buffering another feature.

tic

Registration of geographic control points for a coverage representing known locations on the earth's surface. Tics allow all coverage features to be recorded in a common coordinate system such as Universal Transverse Mercator (UTM). Tics are used to register map sheets when they are mounted on a digitizer and to transform the coordinates of a coverage—for example, from digitizer units (inches) to the appropriate values for a coordinate system, which are measured in meters for UTM.

tolerances

A coverage uses many processing tolerances (fuzzy, tic match, dangle length) and editing tolerances (weed, grain, edit distance, snap distance, and nodesnap distance). Stored in a TOL file, ArcInfo uses the values as defaults in many automation, editing, and processing operations. You can edit a coverage's tolerances using its Properties dialog box in ArcCatalog.

topological association

The spatial relationship between features that share geometry, such as boundaries and vertices. When you edit a boundary or vertex shared by two or more features using the topology tools in the ArcMap Editor, the shape of each of those features is updated.

topological feature

A feature that supports network connectivity that is established and maintained based on geometric coincidence.

topology

1. In geodatabases, relationships between connected features in a geometric network or shared borders between features in a topology.

2. In coverages, the spatial relationships between connecting or adjacent features—for example, arcs, nodes, polygons, and points. The topology of an arc includes its from- and to-nodes and its left and right polygons. Topological relationships are built from simple elements into complex elements: points (simplest elements), arcs (sets of connected points), areas (sets of connected arcs), and routes (sets of sections, which are arcs or portions of arcs). Redundant data (coordinates) is eliminated because an arc may represent a linear feature, part of the boundary of an area feature, or both.

topology cache

A temporary collection of edges and nodes used in ArcMap to query and edit the topological coincidence between features. The cache is built for the current display extent and is stored in the computer's memory.

topology rules

An instruction to the geodatabase defining the permissible relationships of features within a given feature class or between features in two different feature classes. Topology rules are compared against the features in the feature class during the topology validation process, and violations are marked as errors. After the topology validation process, the errors can be corrected by editing the feature class; occasionally, violations of a topology rule may represent acceptable conditions. In these cases, the errors can be marked as exceptions.

tracing

The building of a set of network elements according to some procedure.

transaction

1. A group of atomic data operations that comprise a complete operational task, such as inserting a row into a table.

2. A logical unit of work as defined by a user. Transactions can be data definition (create an object), data manipulation (update an object), or data read (select from an object).

true curve

See circular arc.

undershoot

An arc that does not extend far enough to intersect another arc. See also dangling arc.

union

A topological overlay of two polygonal spatial datasets that preserves features that fall within the spatial extent of either input dataset; that is, all features from both coverages are retained. See also intersect.

username

The identification used for authentication when a user logs into a geodatabase.

See also password.

validate (topology)

The process of comparing the topology rules against the features in the dataset. When you validate a topology, features that violate the rules are marked as error features. Topology validation is typically performed after the initial topology rules have been defined, after the feature classes have been modified, or if feature classes or rules have been added to the map topology.

validation rule

Validation rules can be applied to objects in the geodatabase to ensure that their state is consistent with the system that the database is modeling. The geodatabase supports attribute, connectivity, relationship, and custom validation rules.

version

A version is an alternative representation of the database that has an owner, a description, a permission—private, protected, or public—and a parent version. Versions are not affected by changes occurring in other versions of the database.

vertex

1. One of a set of ordered x,y coordinates that defines a line or polygon feature.

2. A point that joins two segments of a feature. For instance, a square building would have four vertices, one at each corner.

virtual page

The map page, as seen in layout view.

wizard

A tool that leads a user step by step through an unusually long, difficult, or complex task.

work flow

An organization's established processes for design, construction, and maintenance of facilities.

work order

One specific task that proceeds through each stage of an organization's work flow processes such as design, acceptance, and construction in the field.

workspace

A container of geographic data. This can be a folder that contains shapefiles, an ArcInfo workspace that contains coverages, a personal geodatabase, or an ArcSDE database connection.

Index

A

Absolute mode. *See* Digitizing
Active data frame
    defined 229
Adjust
    finishing spatial adjustment 138
Adjustment
    choosing the data to adjust 130
    previewing 137
Adjustment method
    selecting 125, 131, 142
Advanced Editing toolbar 118
Alias
    defined 229
    described 178–181
    feature class 179
    field 15, 179–180
    table 181
Aligned dimension
    defined 229
Annotation
    advanced labeling expressions 39
    creating 194
    defined 229
    feature-linked
        creating 194
        editing 36
    in ArcCatalog 176
Annotation class
    creating 203
Annotation feature class. *See* Annotation: class
Annotation features. *See* Annotation
Arc
    feature classes
        and coverage topology 217
Arc–node topology
    defined 229

ArcCatalog
    creating folder connection 8
    creating schema 173–174
    getting help 6
    mini-browser 177
    previewing data 175–176
    tree 8, 175, 177
ArcEditor
    functionality 2
ArcInfo
    functionality 2
ArcInfo workspace
    defined 229
ArcMap
    adding a topology 111
    and layers 201
    ArcEditor license 45
    ArcInfo license 45
    ArcView license 45
    editing geodatabases 45
    editing shapefiles 45
    licensing for editing 76
    releasing database lock 90
    Selectable layers 243
ArcSDE
    defined 230
ArcView
    functionality 1
Association. *See* Relationships
Attribute domains
    advantages of 2
    coded value domain
        code description 183
        codes 183
        described 183
        in ArcMap Editor 41
    creating 182
    defined 230
    described 182
    mentioned 181
    merge policy
        described 183

Attribute domains (continued)
  range domain
    described 183
  split policy
    described 183
  valid values 183
Attribute Transfer Mapping 151
Attribute Transfer tool 149, 155
Attribute validation rule. *See* Attribute domains
Attributes
  adding 50
  dialog box
    defined 230
  editing in ArcMap 15, 40
  rules. *See* Attribute domains
  tables
    defined 230

B

Behavior 173–174, 186, 193
  adding to features 177–181
Bookmarks 13, 60
Buffers
  defined 230
Building a Geodatabase
  see for more information 6

C

CAD (computer-aided design)
  CAD feature class
    defined 230
  defined 230
  importing features from 85
  loading features 86
  snapping features when loading 88
CASE tools. *See* UML model
Centroid
  defined 230

Check in
  described 230
Check out
  described 231
Check-out
  geodatabase
    defined 231
  version
    defined 231
Circle
  defined 231
Circular arc
  defined 231
Classification 202
Cluster tolerance 205
  default 222
  defined 231
  described 77, 91
  setting 91
  setting for map topology 77
Clustering
  defined 231
Coded value domain 41
  editing attributes with 16
Coincident
  defined 231, 236
Column
  defined 231
Complex edge 40, 190. *See also* Network
    features
Complex junction. *See also* Network features
Composite relationships. *See* Relationships
Compression
  defined 231
Computer-aided design (CAD)
  defined 231
Conflict
  defined 231
Connectivity
  defined 232

Connectivity rules
  advantages of 2
  defined 232
  described 39
  edge–edge rule
    creating 193
    default junction 39, 193, 234
  edge–junction rule
    creating 192
    defined 236
  in ArcMap Editor 36
  mentioned 184, 189
Constraints. *See also* Attribute domains
  defined 232
  edit sketch 54
Construct features
  defined 232
Construct Features tool 117, 120
Contiguity
  defined 232
Control
  defined 232
Control points
  defined 232
  for digitizing 58
Converting data. *See* Importing data; Loading
    data
Coordinate
  defined 232
Coordinate system
  defined 232
  importing for a dataset 211
Copying and pasting features 67
Coverages
  defined 232
  discussion of topology in 217
  loading selected feature classes 219
  mentioned 173–174, 177, 203

Cracking. *See also* Topology: validation
  defined 233
Create new feature
  edit task 49
Creating a topology 204
Creating polygons
  from lines and points 107
Current task
  defined 233
Curve
  creating 54
Custom
  behavior
    defined 233
  feature
    defined 233
  object. *See also* Behavior
    defined 233
Custom behavior. *See* Behavior
Custom feature. *See* Behavior
Custom object. *See* Behavior
Custom rules. *See* Validation rules

D

Dangle
  causes of 97
  dangling arc
    defined 233
  described 93
  tolerance
    defined 233
  types of 95
Data
  defined 233
  integrity
    defined 233
  source
    defined 233
Data dictionary 178
Data frame
  defined 233

Data type
  defined 234
Data view
  defined 234
Database
  defined 234
Dataset 175–176
  creating new 211
  creating topology in 91, 204, 221, 222
  defined 234
  setting precision for 213
  setting spatial reference 212
Decimal degrees
  defined 234
Default
  cluster tolerance 222
Default junctions
  junction type
    defined 234
Default value
  advantages of 2
  associating with a subtype 184–186
  for an attribute 16, 17, 39
Deleting
  features with topology errors 101
Digitizer
  configuring puck buttons
    using WinTab manager setup program 57
  disabling digitizing mode 65
  setting up 57
Digitizer.dll. *See also* Digitizer: setting up
Digitizing
  defined 234
  described 57
  enabling digitizing (absolute) mode 59
  finishing your digitizing session 66
  heads-up 48, 57
  in point mode 61
  in stream mode 62
  mode
    defined 234
  preparing the map 57

Digitizing (continued)
  registering your map 57
  setting control points 58
Digitizing mode
  described 59
Dimension
  styles 42
Dimension feature class
  defined 235
Dimension features
  construction methods
    defined 234
  creating 41
  defined 234
  types 42
Dimension style
  defined 235
Dimensioning toolbar 42
  defined 235
Direct connect
  defined 235
Dirty areas 106
  defined 235
  described 102
  viewing 102
Disconnected editing
  defined 235
Displacement link
  spatial adjustment 124
Displacement links 128
  adding 125, 133, 145
  described 125, 133
  for edgematching 140
  multiple 128
Distance units
  defined 235
Domain
  coded value 16
Double precision
  defined 235
Dragging features. *See also* Moving

E

Edge (topology)
  described 26
  editing with map topology 75, 78
Edge element. *See also* Logical network
  defined 235
Edge features. *See* Network features
Edge–Edge rule
  defined 235
Edge–Junction cardinality
  defined 235
Edge–Junction rule
  defined 236
Edgematching 140
  spatial adjustment method 140
Edit
  coincident parts of features
    with map topology 75
Edit cache. *See* Map cache
Edit session. *See also* Editing; Editing in
    ArcMap
  defined 236
Edit sketch 38, 47
  constraints 54
Edit tasks 47, 49
Editing 173–174, 176, 182. *See also* Editing
    in ArcMap
  map topology with ArcView 76
  selecting the data to edit 52
  setting the current task 49
    for use with a digitizer 60
Editing in ArcMap
  Attributes dialog box 14, 40
  edit sketch 38
  see for more information 6
  Sketch tool 38
  snapping environment 37

Editor toolbar. *See also* Editing in ArcMap
  adding 13
  defined 236
Ellipse
  defined 236
Embedded foreign key 188
Error
  defined 236
  selecting a topology error 97
  topology 19
Error Inspector
  filtering types of error 114
  opening 21, 96
  sorting errors by type 114
Error symbol
  changing 112
Errors
  fixing multiple errors at one time 105
  showing examples for a rule 21
ESRI Annotation Feature. *See* Feature type
Exceptions
  generating a summary of 105
Extend
  advanced editing tool 119
  line features 71, 73
  lines to correct undershoots 99
  multiple undershoots 106
  undershoot topology error 100
Extent
  and precision 214

F

Feature. *See also* Feature class; Feature
    type; Object
  attribute table
    defined 236
  defined 236
  editing. *See* Editor toolbar
  mentioned 173–174
  simple 244

Feature class
  adding to a topology 92, 108
  and geometric networks 189
  and importing data 177
  and subtypes 182
  defined 236
  in ArcCatalog 9, 176
Feature classes
  in a topology 20
  in coverages
    and topology 217
Feature dataset
  and geometric networks 189
  and importing data 177
  creating new 211
  creating topology in 91, 204, 221, 222
  defined 237
  in ArcCatalog 176
  setting precision for 213
  setting spatial reference 212
Feature type
  network. *See* Network features
  topological 246. *See also* Topology
Feature-linked annotation. *See* Annotation
Field
  defined 237
Finish sketch 50
Fix Topology Error tool 99
  fixing multiple errors with 105
Folder connection 175
Foreign key 188
Fuzzy tolerance
  defined 237

G

Geodatabase
  defined 237
  editing with ArcEditor or ArcInfo 2
  feature classes
    editing with map topology 76

Geodatabase data model
  defined 237
Geodatabase topology. *See* Topology
Geography Network
  data source 79
Geometric network 2
  advantages of 2
  Build Geometric Network Wizard 189
  building 189, 189–193
  defined 237
  described 11, 34
  editing 7, 34
  flow direction 191
  mentioned 203
  network weights 191
Georelational data model
  defined 237

H

Heads-up digitizing 48
Hotkeys
  increase productivity with 39
  pan and zoom while editing 80

I

Identity links 128
  adding 137
Importing data
  coverages 177–179
  from CAD drawings 85
  tables 180
Index
  defined 237
Instance
  defined 237
Intersect
  defined 237

Item
  defined 238

J

Junction element
  defined 238
Junction feature class
  creating 191
  sinks 191
  sources 191
Junction features. *See also* Network features
  default 39

K

Key field 188. *See also* Foreign key; Primary
    key
Keyboard shortcut
  described 39
  pan and zoom while editing 80

L

Label point
  defined 238
Layer
  defined 238
Layer files
  creating 201, 203
  described 201
Layout view
  defined 238
Left–Right topology
  defined 238
Line features
  creating 52
  extending 71
  trimming 71
Linear dimension
  defined 238

Links
  types of for spatial adjustment 128
Load Objects command
  adding to ArcMap 86
Load rules
  from rule file 225
Loading coverage data
  for a topology 210
Loading data
  from a CAD drawing 85
Logical network 40. *See also* Geometric
    network
  defined 238

M

Map. *See also* ArcMap
  defined 238
Map cache
  defined 238
Map document
  defined 239
Map topology
  creating 77
  defined 239
  described 76
  editing adjacent features 75
  editing shared edge 79
  editing with ArcView 45
  editing with Topology Edit tool 75, 78
Map units
  defined 239
Master check-out version
  defined 239
Master geodatabase
  defined 239
Measurements
  adding vertices using 53
Merge policy
  defined 239
  setting 183

Minimum bounding rectangle
    defined 239
Modify Features task 73
Moving
    features by dragging 69
    features with a transformation 124
Multipart feature
    defined 239
Multiple Displacement Links
    spatial adjustment tool 135
Multiple errors
    fixing at one time 105
Multipoint feature
    defined 239
Multiuser geodatabase
    defined 239
Multiversioned. *See* Version

N

Natural Neighbor
    spatial adjustment options 131
Network connectivity 36
    maintaining 34
Network features
    edges 190
    junctions 39
Network trace
    defined 239
    mentioned 2
Node
    defined 239
    described 26
    editing with map topology 75
    limiting selection to 83
    moving a specified distance 83
    symbology of 78
Null value
    defined 240

O

Object
    and relationships 187
    defined 240
    mentioned 182
Object class
    defined 240
Object Loader. *See* Loading data
Overshoot
    dangle error type 97
    defined 240
    trimming 98

P

Pan
    defined 240
    to a topology error 115
Password
    defined 240
Pasting
    features. *See* Copying and pasting features
Personal geodatabase
    creating new 210
    defined 240
Planarize
    defined 240
    tool 121
Point
    defined 240
Point mode digitizing. *See also* Digitizing
    defined 240
    described 61
Polygon
    and coverage topology 217
    creating from line features 116
    creating from lines and points 107
    defined 240

Polygon features
    creating 47, 48, 122, 149, 158
Post
    defined 240
Precision
    defaults for a dataset 213
    of dataset
        defined 234
        setting 214
    of spatial reference
        relation to cluster tolerance 91
        relationship to extent 214, 215
        relationship to extent of dataset 205
Preliminary topology
    defined 240
Preview
    spatial adjustment 137
Primary key 188
Projection
    defined 241
Property
    defined 241
Pseudonode 241
Puck. *See* Digitizing
Pull check-in 241
Push check-in 241
Pyramids
    defined 241

Q

Query
    defined 241
Quick-reference
    to topics in other books 5

R

Radius
   defined 241
Rank
   changing for a feature class 223
   defined 241
   of feature classes in topology
      described 92
   setting for a feature class 92
Raster
   defined 241
RDBMS (relational database management
      system) 178
Reconcile
   defined 242
Record
   defined 242
Reference data
   defined 242
Region
   feature classes
      and coverage topology 217
Relate
   defined 242
Related table
   editing values in 14
Relational database management system
      (RDBMS) 178
   defined 241
Relational join
   defined 242
Relationship
   defined 242
Relationship class
   advantages of 2
   cardinality 188
   creating 187–188
   defined 242
   described 10
   editing in ArcMap 15

Relationship class (continued)
   foreign key. *See* Foreign key
   mentioned 9, 176
   origin class 187
   path labels
      backward path label 187–188
      forward path label 187–188
   primary key. *See* Primary key
Relationships
   editing 7
   mentioned 176
Remote geodatabase. *See* ArcSDE
Reshape edge
   topology edit task 81
RMS error
   reducing 59
Root mean square (RMS) error
   and control points
      digitizing 58
Rotate
   features with a transformation 124
   features with the edit tool 68
Route
   feature classes
      and coverage topology 217
Row. *See also* Object
   defined 242
Rubbersheeting
   spatial adjustment method 128, 131
Rule
   adding to a topology 92, 109, 207, 224
   connectivity
      defined 242
   in a topology 20
   loading from a rule set file 225
   topology
      defined 242
Rule set file
   loading rules from 224

S

Saving edits 51, 89
Scaling features 70
   with a transformation 124
Scanning
   defined 243
Schema
   defined 243
SDE. *See* ArcSDE
SDE server 243
Segments
   creating
      parallel to existing 54
      parametric curves 54
   defined 243
Select
   defined 243
Selectable layers
   defined 243
Selected set
   defined 243
Selection anchor
   defined 243
Server
   defined 243
Shape
   defined 243
Shapefile
   defined 243
   editing with ArcView 45
   editing with map topology 76
Shared
   edge 31
Shared boundary
   defined 243
Shared edge
   editing with map topology 79
   moving 26, 31
   reshaping 81

Shared features
  and topology elements 31
  showing 78
Shared geometry
  editing with map topology 75
Shared node
  moving 31, 83
Shared vertex
  defined 243
  moving 80
Shortcut
  hotkeys 39
Show errors
  showing examples for a rule 21
Show shared features 78
Similarity Transformation
  spatial adjustment method 125
Simple feature
  defined 244
Single precision
  defined 244
Sketch
  constraints
    defined 244
  defined 244
  operations
    defined 244
Sketch tool 38, 47, 49, 53
Snap tolerance 190
Snapping 47
  agent 244
  defined 244
  environment
    defined 244
  priority
    defined 244
  properties
    defined 244
  setting the snapping environment 48
  snap tolerance
    defined 244
  when loading CAD features 88

Source field
  for attribute transfer 152
Spatial adjustment 122
  methods 125
  previewing 137
Spatial Adjustment toolbar 123
Spatial database
  defined 245
Spatial domain
  defined 245
Spatial extent. *See also* extent
  and precision 214
Spatial join
  defined 245
Spatial reference
  defined 245
  precision
    relation to cluster tolerance 91
  setting for a dataset 211, 213
  shared by feature classes in dataset 211
  spatial domain 245
Split policy. *See also* Attribute domains
  defined 245
Split-move
  topology node 31
Splitting an edge 29
SQL (Structured Query Language)
  defined 245
Stream mode digitizing. *See also* Digitizing
  defined 245
  described 62
Stream tolerance
  defined 245
  described 62
  setting 62
Structured Query Language (SQL)
  defined 245
Subtypes
  advantages of 2
  and symbology 202
  creating 184–186
  defined 245

Subtypes (continued)
  described 9, 182
  editing 7, 15
  in geometric network 34
  mentioned 173–174, 181
  subtype code 184
  use in topology rules 20
Summary
  of topology errors
    generating 105
Symbol
  defined 245
Symbology 201
  defined 246
Synchronization version
  defined 246

T

Table
  and importing data 178–181
  and subtypes 182
  defined 246
  INFO 173–174, 176, 177–181, 187, 203
Table of contents
  defined 246
Tabular data
  defined 246
Tagged values
  defined 246
Tangent curve
  creating 54
Target field
  for attribute transfer 152
Target layer
  defined 246
  for editing 49
Tic
  defined 246
Tolerances
  defined 246

Topological association
  defined 246
Topological feature
  defined 247
Topology
  adding feature classes 108
  adding rules 92, 109
  adding to ArcMap 94, 111
  advantages of 2
  cleaning up data with 90
  correcting digitizing errors 90
  creating 91, 204, 222
  defined 247
  described 10, 19
  discussed 2, 9
  edge
    defined 235
  editing 7
  in a geodatabase 204
  network topology 36. *See also* Network
    connectivity
  properties 20
  structuring relationships of features 204
  validating 19
  validating current extent 33
  viewing rules 20
Topology cache 29
  defined 247
Topology Edit tool 26, 29
  editing map topology 78
  use of with a map topology 75
Topology error
  discussed 19
  generating a summary of 105
  searching for 96
  symbols for 95
Topology layer 20
  described 95
Topology rule
  adding 92, 207
  creating 90
  creating for subtypes of features 205

Topology rule (continued)
  described 207
  loading from rule set file 224
  using subtypes with 20
  viewing 20
Topology rules. *See* Rule: topology
Topology toolbar
  adding 13
  adding to ArcMap 76
Tracing
  defined 247
Transaction
  defined 247
Transferring attributes
  and spatial adjustment 149
Transformation
  spatial adjustment method 124
Trimming
  lines with overshoots 98
Trimming line features 71
True curve
  defined 247

U

UML model
  setting tagged values 246
Undershoot
  dangle error type 97
  defined 247
  described 99
  fixing multiple 106
  type of dangle error 98
Union
  defined 247
Username
  defined 247

V

Validate
  on creation 209

Validate topology
  and dirty areas 102
  defined 247
  in ArcMap 104, 117
  in current extent 19, 33
  on creation 93, 111, 226
Validation rules. *See also* Attribute
    domains; Connectivity rules
  defined 248
  editing with 7
  mentioned 7, 173–174
Version
  defined 248
  transaction. *See* Transaction
Vertex
  creating
    at absolute coordinates 55
  defined 248
  deleting multiple while streaming with a
    digitizer 62
  moving 80
  moving by dragging 80
Virtual page
  defined 248

W

Win Tab. *See* Digitizer
Wizard
  defined 248
Work flow
  defined 248
Work order
  defined 248
Workbook
  estimated time to complete 4
Workspace
  defined 248

X

XY domain
   defaults for a dataset 213
   extending beyond default 213